RON LUCE

RE·CREATE

SMALL-GROUP STUDY GUIDE

*BUILDING A CULTURE IN YOUR HOME STRONGER THAN
THE CULTURE DECEIVING YOUR KIDS*

Regal

From Gospel Light
Ventura, California, U.S.A.

D1516605

Published by Regal
From Gospel Light
Ventura, California, U.S.A.
www.regalbooks.com
Printed in the U.S.A.

Published in association with the literary agency of
Winters, King and Associates, Tulsa, OK.

Library of Congress Cataloging-in-Publication Data
Luce, Ron.
Recreate : building a culture in your home stronger than the culture
deceiving your kids small group study guide / Ron Luce.
p. cm.
ISBN 978-0-8307-4638-5 (trade paper)
1. Parenting—Religious aspects—Christianity. 2. Children—Religious life.
3. Christian education—Home training. I. Title.
BV4529.L852 2008
248.8'45071—dc22
2008019231

2 3 4 5 6 7 8 9 10 11 12 13 14 15 / 15 14 13 12 11 10 09 08

Rights for publishing this book outside the U.S.A. or in non-English languages are
administered by Gospel Light Worldwide, an international not-for-profit ministry.
For additional information, please visit www.glww.org, email info@glww.org, or write to
Gospel Light Worldwide, 1957 Eastman Avenue, Ventura, CA 93003, U.S.A.

CONTENTS

How to Use this Study 4

Week 1

1. Generation Out of Control 7
2. Are We Not Dreamers? 12
3. The Insidious Grip of Culture 18
4. How We Let the Culture into Our Homes 23

Week 2

5. A Cultural Dashboard for Your Family .30
6. Convenient Parenting = Brainwashed Kids 36
7. Who Owns Their Heart? 41
8. Windows to the Heart 45
9. Communicating Your Values 50
10. A Message in a Memory 56

Week 3

11. A Strong Marriage = Secure Kids 62
12. No Substitute for One on One 68
13. Your Kids Trump Your Career and Ministry 72
14. Show Me Da Money, and I'll Show You What You Value 76
15. Teaching Your Kids to Be Dreamers 81

Week 4

16. One Generation Away from Extinction 88
17. Creating a Church Where Teens *Want* to Come 93
18. Dreamers for God 98
19. Anatomy of a NextGen Church 103
20. Churches that Break the Mold: Double Vision Stories 108
21. Dreamers Always Win (the Culture War) 112

Week 5

22. Paralyzed by the Ordinary 118
23. Winning the PR War 123
24. Who Told Us to Shut Up? 129
25. Making Creative Noise 134

Week 6

26. Teens Who Are Changing Their Generation 140
Conclusion: On the Other Side of Your Dream 143

HOW TO USE THIS STUDY

This guide gives you information on how to break down the 26 chapters and conclusion of *ReCreate* to create a dynamic six-week study. Some chapters are shorter and easier to breeze through, while others offer opportunity for deeper reflection. Leaders, you might have your group use the questions in the workbook simply for group discussion or you might encourage members to write in each answer on their own. You decide the key points you want to discuss, pray through and act on each week.

WEEK 1— Read chapters 1–4 of *RECREATE*
Complete the corresponding chapters in the study guide. End your meeting by doing the Getting Creative section of chapter 1 in the study guide. Discuss, and then commit to your group the one thing you are going to do from the Getting Creative section in chapter 4 of the study guide.

WEEK 2— Read chapters 5–10 of *RECREATE*
Complete the corresponding chapters in the study guide. Have some (or all) in your group share their testimonies per the God's Heart for You section in chapter 5 of the study guide. At the end of the meeting, pair up to pray for each other per the God's Heart for You section in chapter 7 of the study guide.

WEEK 3— Read chapters 11–15 of *RECREATE*
Complete the corresponding chapters in the study guide. Taking direction from the Getting Creative section in chapter 14 of the study guide, plan a game night with your small group. Don't forget to include the kids!

Week 4— Read chapters 16–21 in *RECREATE*
Complete the chapters in the study guide. Decide how your group will act on the project given in the Getting Creative section in chapter 17 of the study guide. End with powerful intercession for the youth of your church.

WEEK 5— Read chapters 22–25 of *RECREATE*
Complete the corresponding chapters in the study guide. Decide how you're going to act on the challenge in the God's Heart for You section in chapter 23 to plan a time to fast with your small group, your spouse or your church and have a time of corporate prayer. Also take time to discuss and pray about the Getting Creative section in chapter 24 of the study guide.

WEEK 6— Read chapter 26 and the conclusion of *RECREATE*
Complete chapter 26 of the study guide. Do the conclusion of the study guide, "On the Other Side of Your Dream," together. Decide how and when you will do the Getting Creative section of the conclusion as a group.

WEEK 1

1

GENERATION OUT OF CONTROL

Have you picked up a newspaper, gone online or flipped on the television today?

If so, did you skim over the deluge of shocking headlines—pop icons committing suicide or getting committed to rehab; underage actresses arrested for driving under the influence; another student turning a gun on his school or on his unsuspecting town? Did you just skim the headline, or did you dig deeper to find out the story? And did you ever stop to wonder why? What's causing this kind of chaos, what damage is it doing to your kids—and to an entire generation—and what can be done to stop it?

As Ron Luce writes in *ReCreate*, behind so much of this madness is a massive *pop-culture machine*. This machine "devours [celebrities] and then spits them out. Lives are destroyed within the machine, as well as influenced by the product of the machine. Then the machine rinses and repeats, looking for the next product to sell and the next person to buy it."

And each life consumed adds more fuel to the fire. "This machine is hungry," Ron says. "It must be fed. It needs more stars to control and exploit . . . They also need fans to sell to. In either case, they do not care about the ultimate effect their machine has on its victims." Who's next?

So, who, you might be asking, are the "they" that comprise this machine? They're the makers and marketers of the media, entertainment and fashion industries, people caught up in a machine of their own making who, in a bid to make more money, sell products and *people* to a gullible public—specifically, a young, unguided public that's entranced by all that Hollywood has to offer.

But there's someone else, someone much greater and more sinister than any moviemaker or MTV executive. He's the machine's ultimate taskmaster and the brutal slave driver behind pop culture's most powerful men and women.

Look up Ephesians 6:12 and 1 Peter 5:8. According to these verses, who's the mastermind behind "the machine"?

_____

_____

_____

_____

If Satan is the one with the agenda, what should be our *first* line of defense against ungodly media and culture?

_____

_____

_____

_____

Look again at 1 Peter 5:8. What, in your own words, does it mean to be "alert" to what's going on in pop culture?

_____

_____

_____

_____

The Branding Age: What Are Your Kids Buying (and Buying Into)?

What are your thoughts when you hear of Viacom boldly proclaiming, "We don't advertise to this generation; we own this generation"? Does it stir up a holy anger in you to rescue kids (and perhaps *yourself*) out of such bondage? Ron points out that the machine thrives by making money off the kids it "provides products" for—unconcerned about how those products may influence or harm those who it is selling to. Such products could be video games, TV shows, music, movies, magazines, clothing and the icons featured in them.

What age is considered the "branding age"?

_____

_____

_____

_____

Think of the teens and preteens in your family or life. What are they interested in? Do you notice any particular patterns forming in what products and brands they like or anything they *have* to have or any celebrity they *have* to keep up on?

_____

_____

_____

_____

Which of the previous are good influences and/or in line with virtuous values? Which influences lend to attitudes and images of impurity, selfishness, disrespect and/or violence?

_____

_____

_____

_____

Have you bought anything for your child or allowed him or her to purchase anything lately that might promote ungodly character? If so, pause for a minute to pray about what God would have you do with that thing and how you should speak to your child about it. Record here what you sense God directing you to do:

_____

_____

_____

_____

The Bible and the Branding Age

In Scripture, we read of several men and women whom God "branded" at a very young age—most likely when they were in their early teens. Before you complete the following questions, read 1 Samuel 16:10-13, Daniel 1 (the whole chapter) and Luke 1:26-38.

As you read about David, Daniel and Mary—ordinary young people whom God used to bring about His extraordinary plans—what does it make you think about the potential for your teen, or the teens in your church?

_____

_____

_____

Why do you think God chose teens as opposed to mature adults in each of these cases? Why might He choose them now?

_____

_____

_____

_____

_____

Now take a minute to ponder the flip side. If God has a penchant for using young people to demonstrate His power and to accomplish mighty things, who do you think the devil will attempt to take down and use to bring glory to his name?

_____

_____

_____

_____

_____

Mooks and Midriffs: Cultural Images of a Generation Out of Control

Ron writes, "Some parts of this culture machine are staggeringly massive. Take Viacom for example; they own Nickelodeon, Nick Jr., MTV, MTV2, VH1, Comedy Central, BET, Logo (the gay channel), as well as other media outlets. They have what they call a 'cradle to grave' strategy. They start when our kids are very young, getting enamored with pop icons as they are baby-sat by Nickelodeon. Soon, they graduate to Nick Jr. and MTV, and their appetite for music and their desire to emulate the clothes, the vogue, and every gesture of the hottest star is kicked into full function mode. They are happy to keep people occupied through every era and epoch of their life, making money as they maneuver them through their entire life cycle."

Do you have, and does your church also have, a "cradle to grave" strategy? If so, what is it? If not, jot some ideas on what you think it ought to be.

_____

_____

_____

_____

Ron also says, "Truly, their industry thrives on the fact that most parents are either irresponsible or completely ignorant as to what the media that is sold to their teens actually contains." Are you aware of what your kids are buying, of what—and *who*—is being sold to them through the media?

_____

_____

_____

_____

_____

_____

_____

It's easy as adults—especially adults who perhaps grew up in middle-class suburban America—to judge the outward appearance and crass behavior of many teens today. The Church often shuns those who are most in need of being rescued. But as ambassadors of Christ, it's our responsibility to snatch them out of the jaws of this machine.

It's time to dream and to encourage your kids to dream. It's time to *recreate* a culture that glorifies God and liberates people. It starts with repentance and prayer, then a commitment to lead by example and disciple and mentor a younger generation, which leads to *acting* on the dreams God has given *you*—and encourage your young ones to do the same.

Getting Creative

Before moving on, take time on your own or with your spouse or study group to get on your knees before God. Since He is the original Creator of culture, He alone knows how to bring it back to life and in line with His Word. He knows how to save those who are being devoured by "the machine" and rescue a generation out of control. Bring what you see in your own family, church and/or city before Him. If necessary, ask Him for forgiveness for any apathy on your part thus far. And then ask Him for a plan, for a *divine* strategy. How is He leading you to help woo hearts away from the machine and into the kingdom of God?

2

ARE WE NOT DREAMERS?

Are we not dreamers?

Can we not dream for the hearts and lives of the young generation in our community?

Are we not dreamers?

Can we not think broadly enough for the youth so that when they get involved in our church and youth ministry, they are so consumed and enveloped with a passionate culture of fervent Christianity that they fall out of love with the things of the world?

Are we not dreamers?

Can we not have a voice in shaping the extensive culture of the entire nation so that our values are winsome and compelling?

Are we not dreamers?

Could dreams provoked by our values actually attract people to our values and to the One who shaped our values, that is, the Lord Himself?

ARE WE NOT DREAMERS?

98 Percent vs. 2 Percent

What goes through your mind as you read the questions above and when you read the following: Can we not dream a dream for our kids and for all the children in our communities? *Cannot the people who follow the Creator of the universe be more creative and compelling* than those who have a creative gift but exercise it in a way that hurts people for the purpose of making millions of dollars? Ron asserts that dreamers control culture, that 2 percent of the population creates what the other 98 percent blindly follow. He says that "dreamers are the ones who spark revolution."

What percent are you—the 2 or the 98? Why?

_____

_____

_____

What kind of revolution could your church—or the youth in your church—ignite in your city if you went forward boldly with the big dreams that God has put in your heart?

_____

_____

_____

If you find yourself among the 98 percent, what do you think stops you from dreaming?

_____

_____

_____

Or, perhaps you have many creative and wonderful things mulling around in your mind—but something's keeping you from actually *acting* on your dreams. What and why is that?

_____

_____

_____

Fear and unbelief often keep believers from stepping out in faith. Read Matthew 25:14-30. What stopped the one slave from acting wisely with the talent his master gave him?

_____

_____

_____

What reward was given to the ones who did something with what they were given?

_____

_____

_____

Look again at David, Daniel and Mary. How does David respond in 1 Samuel 17:20-50?

_____

_____

_____

What does Daniel do in Daniel 1:3-8?

_____

_____

_____

What are Elizabeth's words to Mary in Luke 1:45?

_____

_____

_____

_____

_____

Living for Stuff?

"Our lives are filled with *stuff*," Ron writes. "Stuff to see, stuff to watch, stuff to go to, stuff to wear, stuff to give, stuff to drink, stuff that makes you pretty, stuff that makes you cool, stuff that makes you popular, stuff that makes you sexy, stuff that is fun to do, stuff that is adventurous, stuff that will live your life for you . . ." He says that the culture machine is not just media, it is *stuff*.

Take a few minutes to do some inventory—in your room, the kids' rooms and throughout the house. What kind of "stuff" do you find? How much of it (clothes, toys, movies, miscellaneous) do you think was *sold* to you by crafty marketing? How much of it are things you actually need or thought you'd enjoy before anyone convinced you that you "needed" it?

_____

_____

_____

_____

It's not that having stuff is sin (or that *not* having it makes you more righteous), but "the problem arises when this stuff actually hurts kids because they cannot decipher the lack of positive values in the stuff," Ron says, "or when they don't realize that they are getting addicted to stuff."

Think about how your children spend their free time (or how *you* spend yours). Write here what their main activities are (and yours). How much time per week or day is spent on each thing?

_____

_____

_____

_____

_____

Do you notice any lopsided patterns? Too much time on the Internet, playing video games, watching TV or reading fashion magazines? If the answer is yes, what can you do to encourage your child to get out and play more or spend time on more creative, edifying endeavors?

_____

_____

_____

What can you do *with* your child to inspire time spent well? What can you do for yourself?

_____

_____

_____

_____

What stuff do you and/or your children need to get rid of *today*?

_____

_____

_____

It goes without saying that these industries sell the majority of the stuff they produce, their goods and/or services, by sexualizing the advertisements. Sexual images and innuendoes pervade every arena that Hollywood and pop-culture manufacturers can get their hands on. How is our sexualized society affecting your teens and little ones?

Violence in media has also brought destruction to the innocent. Ron quotes a study from the University of Michigan that notes, "Children's repeated exposure to violent television and video games is the strongest predictor of violence in adulthood," above any socio-economic background or issues of abuse. He goes on to say, "Yet these creative geniuses use their creativity to figure out how to make the blood splatter more realistic on the screen in order to sell more product."

So much of the lyrics of hip-hop music, for example, should be considered nothing short of verbal pornography and violence. Yet, sadly, this is what many youth and young adults tune in to in their cars, online, at parties and on their iPods. Would that more God-fearing dreamers would rise up and take this part of the culture by storm! *And* that more Christian leaders, pastors, business people and parents would rise up and support them!

Acting on Dreams or Enslaved to the Machine?

Ron says that "dreamers own us." Take a look at 1 Corinthians 6:12 and 2 Peter 2:19. It is possible for us to become "mastered" by the dreams of others. The machine of pop culture has enslaved entire societies. Even though some things within the culture might offer us innocent entertainment and might not necessarily be sin, those things, if we're not careful, can become our *substitute* for real life and our kids' substitute for a life fully lived as God intends.

Is there anything in your life or in the lives of your children that you—or they—are mastered by?

_____

_____

_____

_____

"They promise them freedom, while they themselves are slaves of depravity." How do these words from 2 Peter 2:19 apply to current pop-culture producers?

_____

_____

_____

To dig deeper into the previous passage, carefully read all of 2 Peter 2. Journal your reflections on it here:

_____

_____

_____

_____

Joel 2:28 says, "Afterward, I will pour out my Spirit on all people. Your sons and daughters will prophesy, your old men will dream dreams." Will you be one who dreams the dreams of God's heart and inspires "sons and daughters" to do the same? As Ron passionately reminds us, "Now is the time for a new generation of dreamers to arise and unite. It's our choice if we're going to be a part of the 98 percent or the 2 percent. *In what percent will you be?*"

God's Heart for You

Take a look at a young woman whom God gave a radical dream to. Read the book of Esther.

What kind of fears do you think Esther faced?

_____

_____

_____

_____

_____

What were the results of her stepping out in faith?

_____

_____

_____

_____

_____

What did she have to do to prepare for such a step?

_____

_____

_____

_____

_____

How is the Lord calling *you* to be an "Esther" for this generation? To be one who lays his or her life down to save them from the slaughter?

_____

_____

_____

_____

_____

THE INSIDIOUS GRIP OF CULTURE

Chapter 3 of *ReCreate* is alarming and disturbing. As you read it, you might begin to fear that if the kids Ron highlights here—those raised in churchgoing families—could do so much damage to themselves and others, what's to keep your teens from getting wrecked by the world's system? The parents of these children might have thought all was well, not knowing that their kids' secret lives had become a breeding ground for hell. How can we, as Christian parents, pastors, mentors and relatives rescue our young ones from pop culture's insidious grip and guide them into a vibrant, victorious walk with Christ?

Fear Factor

First, let's address fear. How do the following Scripture verses speak to any fear that you might have in your heart regarding your children (or other children you know)?

Psalm 34:4

_____
_____
_____

Psalm 56:3-4

_____
_____
_____

Proverbs 14:26

_____
_____
_____

Matthew 8:26

_____
_____
_____

Philippians 4:6

_____
_____
_____

Our trust has to be in the Lord, above all—not in the Church, a school or even our own good parenting skills. We must lay all fears at His feet. As we seek Him, He'll teach us how to pray for our kids. He'll instruct us how to intercede and do battle on behalf of them and their friends.

How does Ron define the word "insidious" in chapter 3?

_____
_____
_____

What Scripture verse does that remind you of?

_____
_____
_____

Remember 1 Peter 5:8? What is Peter's advice to us?

_____
_____
_____

An Insidious Enemy

Indeed, the devil prowls in search of someone to devour. And, just as a lion in the wild would prowl, he and his angels usually keep themselves hidden as they creep up to their prey. They hide behind the glitz and glamour of Hollywood and behind the façade of "fun," devouring those who are so caught up in it all that they don't even realize they're getting eaten up. Ron puts it this way: "This plan is devised by an insidious *enemy*, whose nature is treacherous and deceitful. The plan is carried out in an inconspicuous manner, seemingly harmless, but actually having a significantly grave effect, like an undetected disease."

How do you think the devil was at work in Matthew Murray's life?

_____

_____

_____

_____

Ron writes that Matthew's secret "inner life was inhabited by turmoil and despair." How could this be possible in a "Christian" home? What might his parents have been able to do to perceive the darkness their son was in? What could they have done to help him?

_____

_____

_____

_____

What about Jamie Lynn Spears? How might her parents have shielded her from Satan's attempts at devouring her childhood and young teen years?

_____

_____

_____

_____

An Awareness Strategy

One way to be aware of what the enemy is up to in the life of your family is to *seek God earnestly*. Many Christians read the Bible and go to church and try to behave as good people, but how many really draw near to God on an intimate level? How many really take their walk with Him to the *next level*? As a believer, regardless of whether or not you're a parent, you must get close to Jesus! "If I only touch his cloak," thought the woman with the issue of blood, "I will be healed" (see Matthew 9:20-22). She knew that she had to get close to Jesus; she had to touch Him to experience His healing power. We also must get close and grab on to Him with everything we have, for our sake and the sake of our children and the children of this generation.

What is your prayer life like? Would you say you (circle one):

- Pray without ceasing? You pray in the morning; you talk to God in your car; you pray in the Spirit throughout the day; you close the night with thanksgiving and prayer.

- Usually take some time during the day to pray and seek the Lord?

- Try to get alone with God for some quiet time at least a couple times a week?

- Sometimes pray on your own?

- Don't even know how to answer this question?

If you aren't satisfied with your answer to the previous question, what do you need to do to make sure you're seeking the Lord daily on a deep level? Do you need to carve out more time? Do you need to talk and pray with someone else, maybe a strong Christian friend, mentor or pastor?

_____

_____

_____

_____

Look up Jeremiah 29:11-13. What does God promise those who seek Him?

_____

_____

_____

_____

According to Ephesians 1:17 what does God want us to have?

_____

_____

_____

_____

Write a prayer of intercession for your children, youth group and/or other kids you care about, committing them to God's care and committing yourself to stand alert for them and protect them from Satan's insidious plans.

_____

_____

_____

_____

God's Heart for You

God not only wants you to be aware and for your family to be protected, He also wants you to be *empowered*. Before Pentecost (see Acts 2), Jesus told His disciples not to leave the city, but to wait until they were "clothed with power from on high" (Luke 24:49, *NASB*). Only by the power of the Holy Spirit were the once scared and scattered apostles able to preach the gospel with boldness and go out and do the things that Jesus did. Only by the power of the Holy Spirit was Peter able to discern that Ananias and Sapphira were lying about their money (see Acts 5:1-10). Only by the power of the Spirit could the young Church survive and grow by the thousands despite intense persecution.

We are no different. Have you been clothed with power from on high? Have you been baptized by the Holy Spirit? Are you walking in the fullness of power, boldness and discernment that God has for you to walk in?

_____

_____

_____

_____

Read the following verses: Luke 24:49; John 1:33; Acts 1:4-8; 4:31,33. Stop now to ask the Holy Spirit to baptize you in His presence and fill you with His power. Ask Him to give you a spirit of wisdom and revelation that you might discern what's really going on with your children and what's really going on around you spiritually. Pray that you might be a bold and powerful witness to a world desperate for Jesus; and that, above all, you might be close to the One who loves you and your family and this generation of young people enough to die for them.

4

HOW WE LET THE CULTURE INTO OUR HOMES

Imagine waking up in the middle of the night to the sound of footsteps outside your home. Imagine peeking through your blinds to see a pair of eyes glaring back at you and hearing the roar of a wild beast just a few feet away. Most of us, thank God, will never find anything fiercer than a squirrel or stray cat in the yard; but, spiritually speaking, something fierce indeed does prowl around seeking entry into your home.

As noted in chapter 1, demonic forces are at work looking for people to devour (see 1 Peter 5:8); and because Satan himself "masquerades as an angel of light" (2 Corinthians 11:14), how careful and diligent ought we be to guard what comes into our homes and the portholes through which it might come?

In chapter 4, Ron analogizes these forces to a terrorist or child predator making himself at home on your couch—and you *welcoming* him to do so. It's the same, he says, as allowing "a TV or computer [to] reside in our kids' bedrooms." He goes on to say that "every time we let unsupervised media into our homes and into our kids' minds, we have invited a terrorist into our home." He's referring not only to TV and the Internet, but to all forms of media and communication, including video games, music, movies, magazines, cell phones and even friends.

Do your children play video games at home (on TV, the Internet or handheld devices)? If so, what type of games are they playing?

_____

_____

_____

How many hours per day do you allow them to play? Do you feel that this is too much time, too little time, or just the right amount? Why?

_____

_____

_____

How many dollars per year on average do you and/or they spend on video games? Do you think that this is a reasonable amount?

_____

_____

_____

_____

Do you know the content of each game? Describe this content below. Do any of the games contain violence?

_____

_____

_____

_____

Do you feel that you should get rid of any of those games today? If so, what steps will you take to make this happen?

_____

_____

_____

_____

MySpace

Ron writes, "Virtual worlds are simply online sites that let you pretend you are someone else while you pursue fake relationships with other people doing the same. It's hard to control. Are the kids making real friends on these sites or are they spending time with predators? What manner of values are they discovering? What kinds of conversation are they having? This is just another example of an entryway flung wide open to a negative part of today's culture."

Do you know if your kids are on MySpace, Facebook or another online "community"? What steps will you take to find out this information? If they do have a page, have you seen the profiles they've put up of themselves?

_____

_____

_____

Do you monitor who your kids are chatting with and what the content of their conversations are? Why is this an important step to take with your kids?

_____

_____

_____

What do you think are the dangers of kids being on such websites?

_____

_____

_____

What are the benefits?

_____

_____

_____

So many teens and young adults are hurting and longing for companionship that it's no wonder such sites have exploded in popularity. The legitimate (and usually subconscious) need behind it all is the need to be loved and to have genuine relationships.

How can we as parents, pastors, mentors and friends help fulfill those needs and teach our children how to build healthy relationships with healthy communication?

_____

_____

_____

Read Romans 12:9. What does this verse say love must be? What are we to cling to and what are we to hate?

_____

_____

_____

Take time to share Romans 12:9 with your kids or the kids/teens that you're mentoring or pastoring. Love them enough to have honest dialogue with them about the dangerous possibilities on specific websites and on the Internet in general. You might want to read them some of the stories from this chapter and ask them how they think the teens involved could have kept out of these situations.

Remember, *you're the parent*. You have authority to restrict access to such sites and thus to the dark culture awaiting your children. And what about their real (not *cyber*) friends? Who are they spending most of their time with? Do those friends have a positive or negative impact on your kids' interests and attitudes? A godly or ungodly effect on the things your child says and does?

In 1 Corinthians 15:33, Paul says, "Do not be misled: 'Bad company corrupts good character.'" Does this mean that you should prohibit your child from hanging out with any kid who doesn't go to church or who happens to let a few foul words slip out every now and then? Of course not; but the point here is to be alert and cautious *and* to be prepared to minister to those friends who are less than good company. They probably got to where they are because of an unpleasant, ungodly upbringing. Perhaps they, too, need a mentor who will love them and encourage them to pursue purity and godly dreams. Perhaps that person is you!

The Text Generation

Reread the "Cell Phone" section in chapter 4 of *ReCreate*. What does Ron caution about children having their own cell phones?

_____

_____

_____

Do your children have cell phones? If so, what features are available to them on their phones?

_____

_____

_____

Again, *you have authority* to limit access and to say what's allowed and what isn't. It's not so that you can be a mean, power-hungry parent, but so that you can protect your young ones from harmful communication and from the evil intentions of others.

So-Called Literature

Technology and media might be the easiest things to recognize as major dream stealers and ungodly influencers, but what about the books and magazines your child or teen reads for fun? Many parents let the devil creep in under their noses in the form of so-called literature. But the likes of Harry Potter and other science fiction and fantasy novels might be nothing more than platforms for glorifying witchcraft and sorcery. It might be impressive that your 12-year-old can read a 1,200-page book, but do you know the content of that book? Often weaved within fantasy and sci-fi are violence, sensuality and demonic expressions. And with "teen" magazines such as *Seventeen* and *CosmoGIRL!* how can it be that the younger version will be pure and wholesome when the adult version headlines lust and sex in every issue?

Many publishers of Christian literature today are putting out hip, relevant magazines and books for youth and teens. Simply go online or to a local Christian bookstore to find out more (you can visit www.regal books.com or www.acquirethefire.com for resources). Better yet, search online with your teens or take them to the bookstore and let them pick out a book, magazine or Bible study that captures their interest.

Music, TV, Movies and Dream-killers

Overconsumption of these forms of media and the products they sell cripple our children's imaginations and creativity. Ron points out that they are not only "absorbing the values of the creators—the dreamers—of these products, but the content of these products is also numbing their own ability to dream." They get numb to things that should shock them and dumb to the wiles of those selling to them.

Have you ever used the TV or a movie (or video games) as a "baby-sitter" for your children? Do you still? What are some of the dangers of engaging in this practice? List several below.

_____

_____

_____

_____

_____

How many hours of media (movies, music, television) do you think your child takes in each day? Is this a healthy amount? Why or why not?

_____

_____

_____

_____

_____

Ron writes, "Every time they watch, listen, and participate for one hour, two hours, three hours, four hours, to a website, a movie, a magazine, their hearts are being taken in by someone else's dream, if only for that short time, and these teens stop creating culture for themselves. The fact is, *we must either be the dreamers or we will be a part of somebody else's dream.*" He encourages us: "Our job is not only to protect them from the maelstrom of a negative and harmful culture, but also to inspire them to be the ones who dream."

Getting Creative

What is one thing you can start doing *today* to help your children (or nieces and nephews or kids in your youth group) become the dreamers of their generation?

_____

_____

_____

_____

_____

_____

WEEK 2

5

A CULTURAL DASHBOARD FOR YOUR FAMILY

As Ron points out, many well-meaning parents want their children to have the things they didn't have. However, all too often that leads to an overabundance of *stuff* and an overconsumption of TV, videos, Internet and pop music. Parents often also don't realize that much of what they didn't have was actually *good* not to have! Pornography, profanity, and violent and sexual content of all kinds just weren't as readily available to those who grew up watching *Tom & Jerry* cartoons and *The Brady Bunch*. And some parents simply let family life morph into what it is without cognitively laying out the ground rules, without teaching their kids how to put values into practice in every area of life. What ground rules have been established in your home? How much TV is allowed? How much time on the computer? It's time to be proactive in protecting our kids from this media onslaught and technological trance!

Media Inventory

The following media inventory is taken from chapter 5 of *ReCreate*. Answer the questions honestly, to the best of your ability, and then take time to evaluate your answers with your spouse or prayer partner.

How many TVs are in your house? _____

How many hours or shows are your children allowed to watch each day? _____

Do you have rules about what your kids can watch? If so, write them here. If not, discuss what they ought to be and then come back and write them here.

_____

_____

_____

How many iPods (or the like) does your family own? _____

Do you know what songs are on your kids' iPods?
❏ Yes   ❏ No

Is there an approval process in your home for acquiring music?
❏ Yes   ❏ No

Have you taught your children proper personal music listening etiquette? If so, what?

_____

_____

_____

Remember Ron's rules: "Our kids knew from the beginning, when they first got CD players, that they could never have headphones on while in the car or when other people were around. We wanted them to realize that this 'personal music device' was not going to dominate their lives or ours. We wouldn't let listening to music substitute for family conversations."

How many computers are in your home? _____

Are there any computers in your children's bedrooms?
❏ Yes   ❏ No

What are your computer-use and Internet guidelines? Describe them below.

_____

_____

_____

Do you know what websites your kids have been on in the last week?
❏ Yes   ❏ No

Do you have Internet protection software on every computer that has Internet access? (Remember: *9 out of 10 kids who regularly do homework on the Internet get an unwanted sexual message online!*)
❏ Yes   ❏ No

Does your child have a cell phone?
❏ Yes   ❏ No

If so, is text-messaging enabled on their phone?
❏ Yes   ❏ No

Is the Internet?
❏ Yes   ❏ No

Is the ability to send and receive photos?
❏ Yes   ❏ No

Do you have an Xbox or other video game consoles in your home?
❏ Yes   ❏ No

If so, where?

_____

_____

_____

_____

What are your guidelines (i.e., hours per day, types of games, and so forth)?

_____

_____

_____

_____

Do you know all of the games your children are playing?
❏ Yes   ❏ No

Is there violent or sexual content in them?
❏ Yes   ❏ No

Gauging the Cultural Invasion

Give some thought to the following questions. How has pop culture influenced your children? Do they have a healthy understanding of what the world is offering them and how to combat it while living within it? Do they know who *they* are as individuals—beloved and treasured by God (and you!) apart from what the media tells them?

How many quotes from a movie have you heard out of your mouth or your kid's mouth in the last week? _____

How many quotes from ads have you said or heard your kids say, and what were the products or services advertised? More important, what is the worldview (mindset) behind those words?

_____

_____

_____

_____

_____

_____

How many times have you heard, "But Johnny does it" or "Johnny's parent's let him do it"? What was it that your child was trying to get you to allow?

_____

_____

_____

_____

_____

_____

As Ron asks, "What happens when all of your family is gathered around a TV program and someone interrupts to get something or accidentally flips the channel? How violent is the response? Does everyone get mad? Do they yell real loud, 'Shut up!'? It may be an indicator that you're so into the media that you value it more than the actual people in the room with you."

Do you find yourself acquiescing to your kids' requests just to get them off your back so that you can have peace in the house? If so, describe one instance.

_____

_____

_____

_____

_____

_____

When is the last time you bought something you didn't really want to buy for your kids after they saw so many ads that they just *had to have it?* Describe one such event.

_____

_____

_____

_____

_____

What would your kids say if somebody asked them, "What are your TV rules?" or "What are the Internet rules in your house?" or "How are they enforced and how are they implemented?"

_____

_____

_____

_____

_____

Do your kids know what your family values are? If not, what will you do to make them better aware of those values?

_____

_____

_____

_____

_____

God's Heart for You

God's heart for you is to engage your children in *your* life as much as you engage in theirs. Your testimony—or personal life story—is important not only for preaching the gospel to others, but also for imparting it to your children. When parents engage children in the details and history of their lives—the good, the bad and the ugly—kids gain a sense of being trusted and of being a greater part of their parents' lives. Have you told your children your story lately? Do they know how and when you gave your life to Christ? Have you shared the struggles you've had and the victories you've won throughout your life? Do they know how you felt the day they were born?

Of course, sometimes our stories require a little "editing" or age-appropriate tailoring, depending on what happened in our past. But you can find a way to tell your story honestly and in a way that's relatable to each child. With the five-year-old, keep it short, sweet and simple. With a 10-year-old, take a little more time to talk and to let him or her ask questions. And with your teen, make a date out of it. Spend an evening talking story and sharing your experiences as a teen, with the struggles and insecurities, hopes and dreams that you had.

Use the space provided below to write your testimony as you might share it with your children.

_____

_____

_____

_____

_____

_____

_____

_____

_____

_____

_____

_____

_____

_____

_____

O my people, hear my teaching; listen to the words of my mouth. I will open my mouth in parables, I will utter hidden things, things from of old—what we have heard and known, what our fathers have told us. We will not hide them from their children; we will tell the next generation the praiseworthy deeds of the LORD, his power, and the wonders he has done. He decreed statutes for Jacob and established the law in Israel, which he commanded our forefathers to teach their children, so the next generation would know them, even the children yet to be born, and they in turn would tell their children. Then they would put their trust in God and would not forget his deeds but would keep his commands.

PSALM 78:1-7

6

CONVENIENT PARENTING = BRAINWASHED KIDS

Proverbs 22:6 says, "Train a child in the way he should go, and when he is old he will not turn from it." *Training* implies time spent. When managers train employees for new jobs, they take time with them, explaining things to them and critiquing their performance. Training for a marathon or college or professional sport requires discipline and an element of self-denial. So, too, training up children requires *sacrifice—*sacrifice on your part and discipline that's sometimes painful for both parent and child. Sadly, many parents abdicate their authority and check out in this area, allowing the media, among other things, to "train up" their children. As Ron puts it in chapter 6, "Somehow we have allowed the media to kidnap and brainwash our kids while they sit in our own living room!"

Baby-sitting and Brainwashing

Ron writes, "Despite all of our best intentions as parents, too many of us have adopted the TV and other technologies as a convenient distraction, and even as baby-sitters, for our kids. Starting at a very young age, we have set them up in front of a TV program, a video or a video game so that we can 'get things done.' Or we regularly appease a child who whines until he gets his way to watch a movie that you know has less than godly values. While it seems harmless enough, you will discover . . . that it is indeed harmful."

Have you ever sat your child in front of a TV show, movie or video game so that you could get things done? Do you use this as a regular practice for keeping your kids occupied and/or pacified? Explain.

_____

_____

_____

_____

Look up Psalm 34:11. What should we be teaching our children? What does the word "fear" mean in this context?

_____

_____

_____

_____

Does that which you're putting before your child teach him or her the fear of the Lord? If not, what could you start doing today to instill reverence for God in your children?

_____

_____

_____

_____

According to Psalm 78:4, what should we be communicating to "the next generation"?

_____

_____

_____

_____

Describe what the video games, TV shows and movies they watch at home are doing instead.

_____

_____

_____

_____

The Path of Least Resistance, or the Way of Sacrifice?

Ron paints a picture of our culture's craving—or addiction, rather—for entertainment and how it has spilled over into our parenting. "Now the path of least resistance," he says, "is having something electronic absorb the dull moments . . . We've grown into a nation that constantly wants to be tantalized. Our kids have grown up in a society where one still moment lacking excitement among a constant stream of entertainment equals immense boredom. From a parent's point of view, allowing the children continuous entertainment also engages a parent's selfishness, because we don't want to hear the kids complaining or whining."

Reflect on the quote above. How much of it is true of you and in your household?

_____

_____

_____

_____

Read Galatians 5:19-24. Perhaps you're not a drunkard or someone who throws fits of rage, but what about "selfish ambition"? Are there any selfish motives in your heart when it comes to parenting, especially as it relates to your kids and the use of media and technology? If so, describe the usual scenario that leads to your using media as a baby-sitter.

_____

_____

_____

_____

What does Philippians 2:3-4 say that we ought to do, and how does it relate to parenting your children?

_____

_____

_____

_____

Ron calls the aforementioned a *parenting of convenience*. You could also call it a parenting of *destruction*. It gives "the Machine"—and the mastermind behind it—open access to you and your kids' lives. That's not to say that every TV show or movie or video game is evil, but that many of them are, and too much time in front of any of them—good or bad—will rob young ones of their ability to imagine and dream and create for themselves.

Are you sacrificing your time and your desires for your children, or are you *sacrificing your children* on the altar of your time and desires?

"It's undeniable that as a parent, you *will* sacrifice *something*," Ron writes. "You can choose to sacrifice up front: time, sleep, career, hobbies while your kids are small. But I guarantee that you will also reap joy and delight as they grow up. You will gain a lifetime of intimately knowing them and the privilege of helping them grow into seasoned, productive, godly adults. *If you don't sacrifice up front, you will sacrifice later.*"

Let the Dreams Begin!

This book and this chapter, however, are not meant to bring a dooms-day message or a list of "don'ts" to memorize; nor are they meant to take you on a guilt trip if you've wandered down the path of least resist-ance. The ultimate goal here is that we would raise and release a gener-ation of dreamers. The goal is to glorify God and expand His kingdom by inspiring our kids and their friends and the kids in our churches to dream big. Remember Ron's encouragement to parents:

> There are masses of other people who would love to entertain them; there are plenty of others who would be glad to take your money for occupying your children's time and keeping their voices from whining. But *you* are the only person who can de-posit your values into them. You're the one who has the oppor-tunity to take them on hikes and walks and campouts. . . . So my encouragement for you now as a parent is this: *Dream a dream for your kids.* What kind of child do you want to see stand-ing before you when he or she is 14 or 15? What kind of young person do you hope for when he or she is 17 or 18?

Take a minute now to answer those questions. What kind of child do you want to see stand-ing before you when your son or daughter is 14 or 15?

_____

_____

_____

What kind of young person do you hope for when he or she is 17 and 18?

_____

_____

_____

And what kind of young adult do you envision when he or she is 21 and 22?

_____

_____

_____

God's Heart for You

"But how," you might be asking, "can I possibly begin to know what to dream—let alone know how to make it happen—for my kids?" Perhaps life is overwhelming you with its various details and ever-faster pace. Perhaps you're a single parent who wants to close this book and cry right now. Or perhaps you're already on top of your game and this is just fueling the fire of the dreams in your heart. Whatever your situation, whether single or married, busy, afraid, scattered, or excited and ready for action, *you can dream for your children and fan the flames of the dreams in their hearts!*

It begins with taking *your dreams*, your hopes and your fears, failings and inadequacies to God *your Father* and laying them at *His* feet. Pour out your heart before Him! Cry out to Him for wisdom—He promises to give it! In Him you'll find all the wisdom, grace, courage and strength you need to sacrifice for your children and to launch them into *His dream* for their lives.

Meditate on James 1:5, Proverbs 1:20-22 and Jeremiah 29:11. Now write out a prayer to God, reflecting on all that has touched you as you read this chapter.

_____

_____

_____

_____

_____

_____

_____

_____

_____

_____

_____

_____

7

WHO OWNS THEIR HEART?

To possess the hearts of your children when they are young isn't terribly difficult—they dote on you—but to keep captivating their hearts at age 10, 11, 12 and on into the teens can seem impossible. As friends influence them, media lures them and their own independent spirit develops, you might feel like you're the last one they want to spend time with. Feeling rejected, you might allow the gap between you and your adolescent to widen. Trying to suture it together, you might make rules that only cause the gap to widen. Or the opposite happens: in hopes of becoming a better "friend" or cool parent to them, you acquiesce to their whims and whining and give them a so-called freedom that only opens the door to more enslavement to pop culture. MTV, MySpace and their peers end up wooing their hearts away from you *and* away from God.

Ron talks about signs—or verbal cues—that we can clue in to in order to better understand where their hearts are at. He calls it "the heart meter." Tune your ears in to listen to what your children are saying, and your eyes in to read between the lines. What do you hear and see?

A Project

Over the next three days, take note of any statements or requests your children make that resemble those Ron writes about in the first few paragraphs of chapter 7. Even take note of nonresponses, those moments when your child is so tuned in to the television or video game that he or she is completely tuned out to you.

Record the names and ages of your children along with your observations:

_____

_____

_____

_____

_____

What signs do you see as you observe your children more carefully? Is there a hint that the culture owns more of their heart than you do?

_____

_____

_____

_____

_____

Ron reminds us of MTV's chilling assertion: *We don't advertise to this generation; we own this generation.* And it's not only MTV, but every other kind of temptation they're bombarded with daily on TV, radio, Internet and at school. To leave it at, "Because I said so!" or "As long as you're under my roof you will do such-and-such" is no longer enough. It might produce temporary, resentful acquiescence, but to really get to the root of the matter and woo your child's heart back to you and away from the world, something more is required of you. That something is the *sacrifice* we discussed in the last chapter; that something is TIME.

Lean into Them

What does it mean to *lean into* your children? "When you start to see signs that your kids care about their friends or what the culture thinks more than what you think," Ron says, "it should be an indicator for you to 'lean into them more.'" He says that leaning in means to draw close to them *relationally*. Kids need validation and affirmation; and if they're getting more of it from sources other than you—friends, music, stuff— take heed. You need to woo their hearts away from those things—and, if you have Christ, you have the power to do it!

Read Romans 12:21. Evil is spewed at your kids all day long—on billboards, on the Internet, TV, radio and "in the air" as spiritual forces seek to tempt them into sin. What are some *good* ways to help your kids overcome this evil?

_____

_____

_____

_____

_____

What does Ron say we must do? What sacrifice must we make to accomplish this?

_____

_____

_____

_____

Ron says that we have to establish "an affinity . . . through a heart-to-heart connection, resulting in their caring more about what we [think], allowing for more opportunity to impart the values that [are] most important to us." How much time, on a one-on-one basis, do you typically spend with your children each week? What kinds of activities do you do?

_____

_____

_____

_____

Dads, if you have daughters, do you take them out on "dates"? If you have sons, do you take them on adventures or have quality guy time with them? What is one simple thing you could plan to do this week with your kids—a separate activity with each of them?

_____

_____

_____

_____

Moms—what special time do you take with your son(s)? With your daughter(s)?

_____

_____

_____

_____

One thing to watch when trying to lean into your kids is that you don't bowl them over with your own stories and stresses. Continuous talking or sharing about oneself does not equal bonding—and often has the opposite effect (think how you feel when you're around an incessant talker!). Sometimes insecurities or being uncomfortable with silence can make us chatty, but remember who you're there for and why. _You're there for your child_ and to work at building a relationship in which they feel important, validated, listened to. And remember: "If you've found that your kids don't really talk and share their heart with you, well, all the more need to lean in. Don't try to probe and provoke them to talk to you right away; just be there doing stupid and fun things with them. Eventually, they will talk. And they really do want to talk; they just want to make sure that you're the one they want to talk to."

You've already started thinking about what you could do with your kds this week. Now list some ideas for special—or casual—dates or outings with your kids. Short on ideas? Refer back to what Ron does with his son and daughters and/or (better yet!) ask your kids!

_____

_____

_____

_____

_____

_____

_____

Your Father's Heart for You

Perhaps you grew up in a home in which you felt insignificant, or you were left to entertain yourself. Perhaps you *feared* interaction with your father or mother. Or perhaps your dreams were crushed or never encouraged by your parents. Sometimes we just don't realize how wounded we were as children or how much we've been wooed by the world until we're parents ourselves! Whatever wounds you carried with you from your childhood into parenthood, God, your heavenly Father, wants to heal them. And in whatever ways you've been won over by the world's system, God wants to redeem your heart for Him alone.

With your spouse or friend or prayer partner, or simply with the Lord Himself, share anything from your past that you feel might be preventing you from parenting the way you want to. Identify anything that keeps *you* from leaning into the Lord, and perhaps from leaning into your children. Ask the Lord to heal and forgive you and equip you to love your kids as He loves them.

8

WINDOWS TO THE HEART

As we discussed in the last chapter, we must be intentional about tuning in to our children, looking and listening for signs of where their hearts are at and for those times when their hearts are *open*. Ron writes:

> When your kids say something that demonstrates *openness*, pay close attention. Openness might come through a question such as, "Mom, do you think I'm pretty?" or "Dad, what do you think I'm good at?" Or it may be a comment like, "I don't think anybody likes me," or any number of statements that linger, awaiting your response. Rather than automatically responding, "Of course you're beautiful," or "Of course people like you," recognize that a window to your child's heart is wide open, and your perception of those window moments can lead to significant life discussions with your child.

Embracing the Inconvenient

Note the words "window moments" in the quote above. Windows to the heart can be more like shutters, flipping shut just as quickly as they peeped open. "Seize the moment," Ron says—seize the moment of opportunity when you can jump through the window to your child's soul. Making excuses because the moment might be inconvenient for you might send a message like, "You're not worthy of my time right now; you're second to my work, ministry, TV show, sleep, etc." The result? Rejection in their heart and, most likely, a wall (not a window) for you to try to walk through later.

But what can you do to be ready for these moments? Sometimes they happen so fast, and the response is so automatic. How can you be prepared to recognize the window and embrace your child's vulnerability at the least convenient times?

Pray. First and foremost, set your desire to engage with your child before God. The Holy Spirit is your Helper and will help you recognize open windows if you ask Him to do so. What does John 14:16-18 state about the work of the Holy Spirit in guiding us?

_____

_____

_____

_____

_____

Commit. Pledge to yourself, your spouse and to God that you are going to be committed to your children in this way. It's vital and something to be vigilant about at all times. What does Proverbs 16:3 say about this type of commitment?

_____

_____

_____

_____

_____

Listen. Genuine listening means *engaging* with eye contact, questions and an ability to keep your comments to a minimum until the appropriate time. What can be learned from 1 Corinthians 13:1-7 about listening?

_____

_____

_____

_____

Love. Ask God to cultivate an even deeper love in your heart for your children — to better grasp *His* love for them. Such love is what took Jesus to the cross for you. Take a minute to meditate on the ultimate love sacrifice as you read Hebrews 12:2 and write your thoughts below.

_____

_____

_____

_____

_____

What to Do When There's a Wall

Ron emphasizes that you can't force open the window to the heart. Whether the heart-window opened once and then shut because of your response (or lack thereof), or has been boarded up with an obvious "Keep Out!" sign for some time, no amount of prying will get you into that window. You might get some information out, but you won't be granted real access to the heart. But there is hope! Ron offers practical wisdom for these situations:

> The window to your child's heart has a much higher probability of opening after you do some activity together that has nothing to do with a serious topic. For example, when you play a nonsensical game or go somewhere fun where your child feels an atmosphere of love and trust and affection from you, the window will probably begin to squeak open by the end of the night, after your time together. Yes, you're tired. You would have been happy for the conversation to come up earlier, maybe over dinner or coffee, or during one of the activities you were doing. But no, your child wants to bring up a topic *now*. The prudent parent will see the crack in the window and take the cue. And even though tired, he or she will ramp up again to go through the window, because open windows are few and far between.

Isn't that the message you'd like to send? A message that tells your children that you care more about them than about your work or ministry, or anything else? A message that says, "You are important, and you have dreams that are important, and I want to encourage you in those dreams!"

Ron talks about being asked to go on midnight runs and to jump into the ocean with his kids when he would have really rather been in bed or basking on the beach. He did those things, however, for the *connection* they offered with his children, even when it was inconvenient. "Even when you would prefer not to," he admonishes, "*do it anyway*, and your child will connect with you on a deeper level and will be more prone to openness with you."

Describe any silly or inconvenient things your kids have asked you to do in the past. *Did you act on those opportunities?*

_____

_____

_____

_____

_____

How did you feel after you went out of your way or out of your comfort zone to connect with your child?

_____

_____

_____

_____

_____

What was your child's response?

_____

_____

_____

_____

_____

How did you feel afterward if you *didn't* do it or didn't listen when your child wanted to talk?

_____

_____

_____

_____

_____

How do you think your child felt?

_____

_____

_____

_____

_____

If Not You, Then Who?

"Whoever your children open up to are the ones who will have the most influence on shaping their heart and life," Ron says. Who, or what, is shaping your child's life the most? If your children are not sharing their hearts with you, then most likely, you're not the one with the most influence. Who hears the deepest part of your child's heart? I hope it's you (and Jesus!).

Have you cultivated the kind of trust in your kids' hearts that will enable them to be vulnerable to you? Remember Ron's words:

> Your kid's heart will be vulnerable to those who are listening to him or her. Is she sharing her heart online on MySpace? It's tragic when a kid blogs his or her pain for all the world to see because Mom and Dad, sitting 10 yards away from where the child sits typing away, are too busy to listen. If you haven't had a heart-to-heart talk with your kids in a while, you need to find out who they're sharing their heart with. But do it in a very subtle way. Start creating opportunities to show tangible love so that perhaps the window to their heart will be opened to you once again.

Getting Creative

What opportunities can you begin to work on to show your child tangible love? What things can you start doing daily to express that? What are some ideas of special outings or activities you can do with each of your children? In creating these opportunities, you're creating keys that could open their hearts.

Feeling afraid and not sure how to go about this? Take your concerns to the throne of God: "Let us then approach the throne of grace with confidence, so that we may receive mercy and find grace to help us in our time of need" (Hebrews 4:16).

9

COMMUNICATING YOUR VALUES

Ron states, "Start actively working with your children at the very youngest age to create a family culture that builds stability, sets expectations and ensures security in their hearts."

If you have young children, list some of the negative, destructive patterns you see in teens around you that you want to steer your kids clear of.

_____

_____

_____

_____

_____

What can you do *now* to keep them on a positive, pure, secure path?

_____

_____

_____

_____

_____

Take a minute before going on with this chapter to pray and ask the Lord for wisdom. He promises to give it to us when we ask! Look up James 1:5 before you pray and be confident in God's promise to you.

Whose Lead Are They Following?

Now is the time to question *who* is really raising your children. Ron asks, "Who is having more effect on your kids, you or the culture?" We can't be ignorant of the pop culture swarming around our children from a very young age. Ron suggests that we need not merely be on the defensive, but that it's imperative for parents to be on the offensive, to be proactive in creating godly culture—a counter-culture to what the world so aggressively markets. And what the "Machine" is marketing is more than just catchy phrases and sensual images—it's promoting, imparting and indoctrinating *values* into kids. And what does the Machine value? Homosexuality, teen promiscuity, extra-marital sex, extravagance, self-indulgence, selfishness, abortion, violence, profanity, drug use, disrespect, and more.

Children are like sponges to the media, unknowingly absorbing its content like water. But we can't expect them simply to "absorb" our values at home. There must be a plan in place for imparting our core ideals to them. The next generation is in *your* hands and in *your* home—how will you help them grab hold of godly core values?

God takes this very seriously. Remember Psalm 78? Not only there, but all throughout the Old Testament, He makes a point to tell His people to pass on His principles to the next generation.

Creating Core Values

So, what are your core values? What do you want to instill in your kids, and what kind of kids do you want to raise? Following Ron and Katie's example, create a list of three to five core values upon which to build your "family name, heritage and practices." Consider what you want the foundation of your family to be and what attitudes you want reflected in everything the members of your family do.

Write your values here:

_____

_____

_____

_____

_____

How will you communicate and discuss these values with your kids?

_____

_____

_____

_____

How will you involve them in the process of making these values part of your family identity? Why is this important when introducing and defining family values?

_____
_____
_____
_____
_____
_____

What Scriptures will you use to back up each one of your values?

_____
_____
_____
_____
_____

Looking back at how Ron and Katie "unveiled" and continued to promote their core values, jot down any creative ideas you have for your own family.

_____
_____
_____
_____
_____
_____

Putting Your Values into Practice

Ron says that these core values ought to answer *why* to every rule we have and every action we do. Instead of saying, "Just do as I say," we should tell them *why*—because it is one of our core values that came straight from the Word of God. Do you see your core values at work in every aspect of your life? Are you living them out all the time, even when the children are not around? Even Mom and Dad are held accountable to the family standards. Ron writes:

> In order to make core values meaningful, you have to be able to confront each other in the family on any violation of the con-

tract. This is an area that some parents do not want to hear about! There will be times when we, as parents, violate a core value. When we do, we either need to be quick to confess it to our kids or to acquiesce if they confront us about it, and say, "You're right, please forgive me." *It's very important that you do not act as if you are perfect.* If you want your kids to respond in a positive way to the family core values when you confront them about it, then you need to model the values.

Read James 1:22. How can we apply this to our core values?

_____

_____

_____

_____

_____

_____

First Timothy 4:16 says, "Watch your life and doctrine closely. Persevere in them, because if you do, you will save both yourself and your hearers." How might we damage our young "hearers" if we get slack in our "life and doctrine"?

_____

_____

_____

_____

_____

Integrity to practice all that we preach and enabling our kids to confront us (respectfully) when we fail is essential. "This becomes the foundation for family trust and confidence," Ron says. "It's who you are."

Friends and Mentors

"No matter how good your parenting is," Ron asserts, "your kids get tired of hearing only from you. But when there are other people around your kids who have the same values, they become an echo to your values."

What friends, mentors or family members do you want your child/children spending more time with so as to hear "echoes" of your family values from them?

_____

_____

_____

_____

_____

_____

If you're not a parent—or even if you are—who might you be an "echo" to?

_____

_____

_____

_____

_____

_____

Then there are those whom you don't want your child to be with—those who echo too much of the culture for your child's good. You don't want to alienate neighborhood and school friends, but you do want to use wisdom and discretion. Ron recommends only allowing sleepovers with a select few:

> We made a decision when our kids were small that they could not spend the night at any friend's house. We modified that rule a little to say that they could stay the night at the houses of _covenant friends_. Covenant friends are parents with whom we have a relationship and know that they are raising their kids with the same values we have.

Who would you identify as your "covenant" friends?

_____

_____

_____

_____

_____

At the homes of which families will you allow your child to spend the night?

_____

_____

_____

_____

_____

Your Values and the Media

Do you talk with your children about what you see on TV? If an embarrassing scene or flagrantly provocative song comes on, do you turn the channel as fast as you can and then laugh it off, or do you take time to discuss it (and, of course, turn it off or change the channel!)? How do you help your children see how such things violate *their* core values and the Word of God? Even ideas that pop culture conveys about love are important to address—lest your child believe the lie that love is the lust that rap artists talk about, or the impulsive romance scenes flashed on the big screen. Reflect on what Ron writes at the end of chapter 9:

> If you want a fighting chance of instilling moral fiber in your young people, it is going to take some thought. They will not accidentally pick it up without a word from you. So instead of your kids being a blank chalkboard for the world to write its values on, fill them with truth and help them buy in to the values from the Bible that will give them the best chance for a great life.

The Father's Heart for You

In light of God's love for you, pause a moment now to pray for your children. Pray for the core values you've instilled in them—and for the Word of God to be protected and bear fruit in their lives.

10

A MESSAGE IN A MEMORY

What are your fondest memories as a child? What about core values comes attached to those memories? For instance, you might flash back to long summer days at the lake with your family, which helped instill in you the importance of togetherness or of having fun together as a family. Or maybe your past wasn't so pleasant and the first memories and messages that pop up are those of anger and resentment or of wishing your parents spent more time with you.

Ron says, "Bitter or hurtful memories can become part of the foundation on which children reflect for the rest of their life." Parents have the power to "shatter a tender childhood" if not careful. But parents also have the awesome privilege of making a childhood wonderful as well! Which do you want to be true of you? What kind of memories do you want to build in the heart of your child? What kind of family legacy do you want to impart to them?

Look up Ephesians 6:4. What does it mean to "exasperate" your children?

_____

_____

_____

The *New American Standard Version* of the Bible translates it "provoke your children to anger." Can you think of a time when yo*u provoked* your child to anger?

_____

_____

_____

Did you notice how long it took for your child to recover from that incident?

_____

_____

_____

Perhaps you didn't provoke, but you reacted in anger to something your child did. Ron warns:

> A parent's reaction to a child's actions is the bulk of what stays in the child's memory. If you erupt in fiery anger, the *last thing* your child will remember is what he or she did, the meaning of the words you shouted or how they *should have* reacted. Children will, however, remember that livid look on your face, the harsh tone of your words or the humiliation they felt.

Asking Forgiveness

We all blow it with our kids at some point. As parents, it's important to set a standard of humility and forgiveness within our family. Pride or a sense of not wanting to appear wrong or weak before your child could prevent you from doing this, but you have to rise above that. Rather than branding bad memories in your kids' minds, turn hurtful situations into lessons and family growth by humbling yourself and asking your child for forgiveness. Ron says, "You can turn the whole memory around based on the heartfelt sincerity of your apology." Kids know if it's sincere or just a perfunctory apology (just as you know when they apologize to appease you, rather than to make right a wrong done).

Look again at Ron's example of apologizing to his kids on their vacation. He not only asked his family for forgiveness, but he also literally did a "do-over," got on his knees and told his daughters how much he loved them. He explained to them that his anger sprang out of his love, but that his response wasn't right. They "started over" on their vacation and had a great time.

"There is definitely a way to redeem negative interaction with your children," Ron says, "if you remember that you are not just living your life, but you are also creating memories that will replay inside of hearts and minds forever and ever." Read Nehemiah 9:17, Daniel 9:9 and Ephesians 4:2-3 and reflect on the Lord's heart for humility and forgiveness.

Creating Good Memories

Ron says that good memories are "the hard drive from which [our kids] will recall their lives" and he makes a very conscious effort to create those memories with his own family, all the time. He started when his children were just babies. Going on trips, he didn't leave all of his kids at home with Mom or with a baby-sitter—he took them with him! Even before they were toddlers he found ways to show his kids what an integral part of his life they are. (How many businessmen do you know who are changing diapers in between meetings?!)

Look at the list of some of the memories Ron has made with his kids. Describe here the last four or five times you've intentionally tried to create memorable moments for yours:

_____

_____

_____

_____

Now write out some ideas to implement *this month*. (And remember, they don't have to be huge events; they can be as simple as a picnic at the park or as silly as wearing wacky hats to the bowling alley.)

_____

_____

_____

_____

_____

Another great thing Ron mentions is *family night*. The Luce family had theirs once a week. Ron writes, "Each family member got to choose an activity on their week, whether it was watching a movie, eating out or playing a game. Our challenge was to find something creative and 'outside the box' that would not just be a fun activity, but would also create a great memory."

Get your kids in on it! Let each of your kids plan a night they can get excited about and that, together, you can make special for the whole family. Again, there is sacrifice involved. Family night might not be convenient and might not be something you particularly like each time, but you're doing it for your kids. Not only will you be making memories, but you will also be creating the unique culture of your family and cultivating imagination in your kids.

Making Teen Years Memorable

Unlike Jewish and Arabic cultures, Western society doesn't make much of *rites of passage*—celebrating certain years of a young person's life as they pass into adulthood. As a family, however, you can create something special that commemorates a coming of age, like Ron did with his kids.

When Hannah turned 13, we made an important statement to introduce her to such a special time in life. We wanted her teenage years to be exciting, full of life and memorable, not just a bunch of stressed-out, hateful experiences to get through. Every year we did something special and exciting to celebrate. Then our second daughter got the same gift when she turned 13.

Turning 13 was a special "rite of passage" for our girls. We just completed celebrating Cameron's thirteenth birthday. His special time will be a little different, because he's a boy. With the girls, we took them on a date for a weekend of play and fun. But we also talked about some serious things and then presented them with a purity ring (a ring that signifies a pledge of sexual abstinence until marriage).

What can you do to celebrate your teen and acknowledge that he/she has entered a new and important season of life?

_____

_____

_____

_____

_____

If you were to pick a theme verse for your child's rite of passage, what would it be? Jot down some ideas here.

_____

_____

_____

_____

_____

_____

Your Commitment Communicates Their Value

Reread the last segment of chapter 10 in *ReCreate*. What would you have done in Ron's situation?

_____

_____

_____

_____

How did his commitment to his daughter communicate value to her?

_____

_____

_____

_____

_____

Ron writes, "Had I said yes, I would have communicated to Charity that going with this guy was more important than the date I had made with her." Instead, he gave her the message: "You are more important than all the notable Christian leaders I could be spending time with."

He goes on to say, "Those kinds of memories are the ones that make our kids secure and open their hearts toward us. Those choices make them feel valued, which in turn increases their pliability when we attempt to shape them and pour our values into them. In every memory, there is a message. Make sure the memories you leave your kids contain the right kinds of messages."

God's Heart for You

Going back to the beginning of this chapter, if the memories you touched on from your childhood made you wince rather than smile, know that your heavenly Father wants to redeem those memories. Imagine the cross. See Jesus taking your bad memories and childhood heartaches with Him to the cross. See them nailed there, crucified with Him.

Now see Him resurrected, glorious, alive. See Him presenting you with a gift, a gift of how much He loved you as a child and how much He loves you now. Feel His embrace. Be healed of your bad memories and start creating beautiful new memories *today*!

WEEK 3

11

A STRONG MARRIAGE = SECURE KIDS

"The culture of a home emanates from the relationship between husband and wife (for children, that's Mom and Dad)," Ron asserts in this chapter on how your marriage affects your children. "If we really want a chance at creating a culture in our home that is stronger than the culture of the world," he says, "we have to pay attention to the health of our marriage relationship."

It is from that strong marriage relationship that children feel most secure. A stable, loving, dream-inspiring home life begins with a man and a woman who work hard to create it. As with raising children, maintaining a thriving marriage requires sacrifice. It means laying down your rights and desires to grow in unity with your spouse and to be a blessing to him or her (and, thus, to your children).

What kind of marriage does God want you to have? Write down your thoughts after reading each Scripture passage.

Proverbs 5:18-19

_____

_____

_____

Song of Solomon 4:9-10

_____

_____

_____

Malachi 2:14-15

_____

_____

_____

It Begins with God

Psalm 128 gives us a beautiful picture of a happy, prosperous family: a wife who's "like a fruitful vine" and children who are "like olive shoots" around the table. But the foundation of such a family is the *fear of God*. "Thus is the man blessed who fears the LORD" (v. 4). It is God's covenant love toward us, and our love back to Him, that enables us to love our spouse and our children the way He intends. Having problems in your marriage? Or maybe you're just having a hard time communicating with your spouse? Then take some time to communicate with God. Establish a strong relationship with Him that you can build your marriage and family upon.

Time Together

Ron stresses the importance of continually pursuing your wife or husband—letting that person know how much you love and want to spend time with him or her. Don't let the busyness of life keep you running in opposite directions! Make a concrete plan for how and when you will spend time together in the midst of a busy week.

What will you do to ensure time together each day?

_____
_____
_____
_____

Each week?

_____
_____
_____
_____

Each month?

_____
_____
_____
_____

Each year?

_____

_____

_____

_____

Do you have a weekly date night? What kind of activities?

_____

_____

_____

_____

If not, why not?

_____

_____

_____

_____

What creative, fun or romantic ideas can you come up with for the next month of dates? Remember to keep your *spouse's* interests in mind—what would he or she love to do, even if it's not so appealing to you?

_____

_____

_____

_____

Do your kids physically see you spending time together? Do they see your spouse taking priority over them in your life? Ron's advice:

> It's important for children to see that they are not the center of your universe. If they are the center of your universe (which is common thinking of parenting romanticized), they control your world. They get you to do anything they want. What?! My spouse is more important than my kids? It might sound harsh or heartless, but the fact is, kids feel secure when they see a team of a mom and a dad who love each other and are committed to each other. The kids feel fine being priority number two.

A Unified Front

Unity is essential. If you disagree with your spouse, do so in private. Let your kids see a unified front—Mom and Dad in agreement with no division between them. In so doing, not only will you keep your kids from pitting one parent against the other, but you'll also keep the devil out (see Ephesians 4:27).

Have difficult discussions in private, where the kids can't hear you. And choose to be mature, not seeking for your child to affirm your point of view over your spouse's. Ron says, "Even if you are the one who acquiesces and does not get your way, you still win, because as a team, you are both deciding to go the same direction."

He also admonishes couples to stand up for each other. "We always made each other look good for our kids," he shares. "There is no advantage to the child feeling like one of you is the favorite parent." What a wonderful feeling to know that someone's always got your back and that your spouse is your greatest ally!

Read the following Scriptures (with your husband or wife, if possible). Write down and/or discuss how you can apply each to your marriage.

Romans 15:5

_____

_____

_____

_____

1 Corinthians 1:10

_____

_____

_____

_____

Philippians 2:1-5

_____

_____

_____

Proverbs 21:19

_____

_____

_____

_____

_____

Remember: "A solid, thriving marriage relationship builds a culture of trust and confidence so that you can pour your values into your children and they will receive your teaching, because they see the benefits in your own marriage."

Parenting and Leading *Together*

Do you have a parenting philosophy and a plan you both agree on? Do you have mentors or wise parents of your own that you look to for support and advice? Do you know that you can impart values to your children not only in how you discipline them, but in how you discipline them *together*, as a team? Remember Ron's encouragement: "You are a refuge for each other so that you can lead from a position of strength."

Good family leadership also requires *integrity*. "The way you conduct your relationship with your spouse adds to or detracts from your moral authority with your family," Ron states. "Do your children see what you say reflected in how you live? And do they see the two of you living it out together? We would all like to say, 'Do as I say, not as I do.' But that is exactly what Jesus said about the Pharisees. The truth is, children look to us and do what we do much more than they do what we say. As the saying goes, 'More is caught than taught.'"

Examine your life—do you see any discrepancies with what you're trying to teach your kids, what you're saying to them and how you actually live?

_____

_____

_____

_____

_____

Are there things that you're telling them not to do (such as swearing, using God's name in vain, shouting, lying) that *you* yourself are doing?

_____

_____

_____

_____

_____

_____

According to Matthew 25:23, what is Jesus' response to this type of behavior?

_____

_____

_____

_____

_____

God's Heart for You

God's heart for you is to have a fruitful, fulfilling marriage that brings glory to Him, joy to you and your spouse, and peace and security to your children. Go ahead, romance your wife! Be passionate about your husband! Set an example for your children that goes so far beyond what the world has to offer that they will never want to emulate "Brangelina" or "Bennifer" (or any other Hollywood über-couple).

So take some time this week to sit down and have a deep heart-to-heart with your spouse—to tell your spouse what you love about him or her and to encourage each other to be the best parents you can be. Not married? Then spend some extra time with the Lord, linger with Him and let Him love on you. As He pours into you, and you pour into your spouse, your children and other children you know, you will reap the benefits.

12

NO SUBSTITUTE FOR ONE ON ONE

"There is no substitute for one-on-one time with your children, on a regular basis," Ron writes. "It's easy to think, *I can just do a whole family outing*. Family vacations and dinners are great. Playing as a family is great." *But*, he reminds us, "Each person has his or her own challenges, frustrations and insecurities. When you get one on one and talk, you optimize the opportunity to truly engage your child's heart at a deeper level."

How much one-on-one time, on average, do you get with each of your children every week? Do you feel this is enough? Too much? Why or why not?

_____

_____

_____

_____

_____

The truth is that every child—every person—is an individual and needs to be treated as such. Every child needs to be acknowledged uniquely for who they are; each child needs to be heard and invested in. Why is one-on-one time with each child so vital?

_____

_____

_____

_____

_____

Creating Opportunities

Ron encourages you to start this when your children are very young—he started when his kids were still infants! Even taking your kids with you on business trips or on little errands around town are great ways to cultivate one-on-one conversations. Inconvenient? Yes. A sacrifice? Often. Foolish to the world? Probably. Necessary to the growth and confidence of your child? Most definitely. Worth it? Absolutely! Ron makes a crucial point:

> A parent's common excuse is, "I just don't have time to spend one on one." My answer to that is, "Do you have time for therapy?" Do you have time to take your kids every week for three years to somebody who can help them and talk through issues with them? So many of life's "common" problems are solved by having a sounding board, and you want to be sure that you're that sounding board for your child.

Ron also says, "When we get into a regular rhythm of meeting with our kids, it doesn't always have to be intense. But you must proactively create an environment where they will feel like they want to share their heart. If you don't ever set that up, the heart-sharing will never happen."

Make It Happen!

Fill in the chart below with the name of each child, the activity you're going to do with him or her (or a planned trip), and the date or day of the week (this week!) you'll do it:

NAME	ACTIVITY	DAY/DATE

Look up Psalm 127:3 in your Bible. The *NASB* translates it: "Behold, children are a gift of the Lord, the fruit of the womb is a reward."

In light of this, how ought we to view the one-on-one time we get with our kids?

_____

_____

_____

_____

Listen!

"Be careful to guard yourself from the temptation to jump in and correct, coach or fix everything," Ron warns, "Let your child talk!" Think about how you feel when a friend, family member or co-worker steals your thunder. Someone who always butts in and would rather eulogize than really listen to what you have to say is not someone you really want to be around. Don't become that person to your children! James 1:19 says, "Everyone should be quick to listen, slow to speak and slow to become angry." That's good advice for parents to follow!

"We as parents want, and need, to be *the relational center of our kids' life*," Ron says. "We don't want them sharing their hearts with friends, with a blog or in a gang."

List here some things you should practice to ensure you're really listening to and engaging your child (e.g., keep eye contact, turn off the computer, turn work thoughts "off").

_____
_____
_____
_____
_____

List three or four activities your child would enjoy that might bring his or her heart out (do the list for each child you have).

_____
_____
_____
_____
_____
_____

Time and Love

"All it took was time and love," Ron writes of the transformation he saw in one former Satan worshiper. He didn't preach at the kid; didn't avoid him; didn't just plop him in church and expect him to come around. No, he found meaningful and fun ways to spend time with and love on him.

First Corinthians 8:1 says, "Knowledge puffs up, but love builds up," or, as the *NASB* puts it, "love edifies." How beautiful is that—that we can "edify" our children? You've probably heard the age-old adage, "People don't care how much you know until they know how much you care"— how true it is with kids! Talking at them will only drive them away like a fierce wind; avoiding them will only draw them to less trustworthy sources for love and support; engaging and listening to them will unlock the windows to their heart and give them a safe haven inside the window of yours.

God's Heart for You

Meditate on Psalm 139. What does this psalm tell you about God's heart for you?

_____

_____

_____

_____

_____

What do 1 John 3:16 and 4:10 tell you?

_____

_____

_____

_____

_____

_____

13

YOUR KIDS TRUMP YOUR CAREER AND MINISTRY

When you come home from work each day—or when your work day is done, if you're a homemaker or working from home—what's the first thing you do? What's your routine in the evening? Are you quick to engage with your family or do you shut down in front of the television or with a pet project around the house? Do you have dinner together as a family? What do your kids usually get from you in the few hours before they go to bed?

Ron shares about how he once passed up an opportunity to meet with our country's president when he was on a family vacation. It seemed like an ideal opportunity, something that might never come along again, and something Ron really would have liked to do, but he let it go. He said no to the invitation to meet the United States Commander in Chief, and yes to his commitment to his family.

Ron states, "There may or may not have been another opportunity to meet with the president, but there would never be another opportunity to raise my kids. There would never be another opportunity for this vacation. I had one chance to leave an indelible mark in their mind of the value that I place on them."

Value Openly Expressed

How much do you value your children? What kind of self-worth do you think they have because of how you treat them? The decisions we make every day—whether to spend time with family or in the pursuit of personal advancement (or even to spend it ministering to others)—will impact our kids forever. This isn't to say that we should stay home from work, or never accomplish personal goals or become successful because we're wrapped around our children; but that there has to be balance. How we spend our time reflects how much we value our family. What messages are you sending to your children with the time you spend—or don't spend—with them?

Think of something you were involved in when you were little, maybe it was a sport or ballet or a talent show. How did you feel when your parents showed up to watch you play or perform? Or, if one or both of them didn't show, how did that make you feel?

_____

_____

_____

Now think of a time when you were in high school. How did you feel when your parents cheered you on from the sidelines (or when they didn't)?

_____

_____

_____

What kinds of messages did these moments with or without your parents communicate to you?

_____

_____

_____

_____

As an adult, do you recognize any lingering effects, either positive or negative, that these moments and messages had on you?

_____

_____

_____

_____

Proverbs 31:28 says, "Her children arise and call her blessed; her husband also, and he praises her." Though this passage speaks specifically of a noble woman, ask yourself, whether you're a mom or a dad, what it would take for your children to love and respect you this much? Are you pouring into them and honoring your commitments to them so much that one day they will rise up and call _you_ blessed?

Decide _Today_ Your Commitment Tomorrow

Ron advises that we decide in advance how we will spend our time so that when opportunities arise for ministry, job advancement, time with friends—any opportunities that conflict with family time—we will know how to respond. "All of us are busy people," he writes. "If you have a career, are involved in ministry, or have a desire to succeed in some kind of endeavor, there are always going to be other things to do to keep you away from your kids. You have to make a decision *in advance* that your spouse and children are more important to you than your career and/or ministry. Period!" Opportunities come and opportunities go, but *you will never get a chance to raise your kids again.*

What are the non-negotiables in your life? What are the things you've decided (or are deciding now) that you're not going to miss?

_____

_____

_____

_____

Look at your calendar and check with your kids' academic and sports schedules (together with your spouse, if you're married). List the events such as birthdays, your anniversary, performances, games, etc., that you must plan for this month, this quarter and this year. Plug them in to your planner right now, highlight them, set an alarm a few days before, if you need to, and commit to being there!

Determine that you will not use the words "But I meant to be there!" or "I meant to remember." Ron says that "when we say, 'I really wanted to be there but . . .' we are sending a message that we didn't want to be there as much as we wanted our career or our ministry." That sends a strong message to our kids of what is more important to us. As Ron and Katie once decided, we must determine what kind of marriage and family we desire and make everything else revolve around that.

God's Heart for You

Spend a few minutes reading and pondering Psalm 127. What do verses 1 and 2 communicate about God's provision for you?

_____

_____

_____

What does the psalmist say that toiling day and night is? Is it worth it in light of what God's already providing for you?

_____

_____

_____

_____

_____

Note that right after the writer admonishes the reader not to spend so much time and energy on work, he turns his attention to children. What does he say that "sons" (children) are like?

_____

_____

_____

_____

_____

Arrowheads take time to sharpen and hone; their shafts have to be straight and stream-lined to fly through the air effectively and strike the designated target. Why would God make this analogy between sons and arrows?

_____

_____

_____

_____

Think of yourself as a warrior whittling away at arrows that you will use to pierce the heart of the enemy. Time is of the essence; quality is crucial. Would you just find the sharpest rock you could and tie it to a stick because an opportunity arose to go play ball with friends or meet with someone important? Do you think the arrow you spent five minutes making would do much in battle? Meditate on that as you consider your involvement with your children. God has given you the awesome responsibility of training them, sharpening them, preparing them to be arrows in His hand. How far and fast do you want your kids to fly? Do you want them to hit the mark? Do you want them to succeed? Then sacrifice the time now to make masterpieces out of them; take the time now so that you might release them later with joy and pride as sharp arrows of light into a dark world.

14

SHOW ME DA MONEY, AND I'LL SHOW YOU WHAT YOU VALUE

What do your money receipts say about you? If you were to keep the receipts of every transaction you made and the money you gave for two months, what story would they tell? What would be reflected about what you value? How you spend your money says a lot about you! Ron writes, "What you spend your money on reflects what you think is important. We either invite or repel the world's culture with every dollar we spend."

What Teenagers Spend on and What We Spend on Them

Proverbs 29:15 says, "The rod of correction imparts wisdom, but a child left to himself [the *NASB* says "gets his own way"] disgraces his mother." Children and teens who get to buy whatever they want or who get everything they want bought for them are—you guessed it—*spoiled*. Their attitudes and behavior become very selfish and indulgent and end up bringing shame and heartache to their parents.

Helping children learn how to spend money wisely prepares them to be responsible adults. And teaching them how to *save* money is a bigger blessing than any iPod could ever be! They might not realize that when they are 8, 12 or 16, but when they're 32, and living debt-free, they will be very grateful. Toys bring temporary pleasure; discipline and godly contentment bring long-term peace.

Study 1 Timothy 6:6-10. What do you learn from this passage about the deceitfulness of greed and the damage it can have on your kids?

_____

_____

_____

_____

Verse 9 says, "People who want to get rich fall into temptation and a trap and into many foolish and harmful desires that plunge men into ruin and destruction." What kind of "ruin and destruction" have you witnessed in the lives of those who get or buy whatever they want?

_____

_____

_____

_____

Many a pop icon falls into this category. Who can you think of who was once at the top of the charts or was everyone's favorite celebrity, but now has fallen from grace and become the laughingstock of gossip media?

_____

_____

_____

_____

Ron says, "Our desire to give our kids more than what we had when growing up can lead to their absorption with the media that destroys them." How do you think giving your children their own cell phones, iPods, TVs, computers or other major "toys" could "destroy" them?

_____

_____

_____

_____

What do you think are appropriate ages for giving—or helping your children to buy— each of these things? Why?

_____

_____

_____

_____

How is it a "blessing" to your teen to make him or her save up for and buy these things himself, or at least to pay for half?

_____

_____

_____

_____

RECREATE SMALL-GROUP STUDY GUIDE

Ron also remarks that "The time they spend and the values they learn from the media contraptions you bring home will actually put you farther away from having a deep relationship with them. Your desire to give them what you never had may turn out to be a curse and drive you farther apart as a family."

Do you recognize any brick walls of communication between you and your children due to a media/technology invasion in your home?

Distracted or Drawn Together?

Are you sending any conflicting messages to your children by what you say versus what you buy? Do you say you want quality family time but then go out and purchase a new Play Station 2 or plasma TV? "We need to think carefully about the impact of the dollars we spend," Ron admonishes. There has to be a connection between what you say and what you do. As we've discussed in other chapters, you have to be intentional about the time—and the quality of the time—you spend with your children. If you set up your latest toy in the middle of the living room, your kids will become intentional about spending time with *it* rather than you.

What about the good ol' fashioned way? What about playing games? Ron suggests breaking out the board games and card games and corny old '70s games that make you laugh and think and talk.

What games do you have in the house that you could pull out for your next family night?

_____

_____

_____

_____

What's your favorite board or card game? _____

_____

Your spouse's? _____

_____

Your children's? _____

_____

It's Okay to Say No!

"Just because you can afford stuff does not mean that you should buy it for your home, or for your children," Ron says. Too often, parents buy what they *can't* afford—on credit—bringing trouble in more ways than one.

Don't worry about what your children will think! The devil wants you to be afraid that they won't like you or that they'll become rebellious if you don't give in; but the Bible says that the fear of man is a snare, but that the one who trusts the Lord is secure (see Proverbs 29:25).

"Owning every toy that has been invented is not the path to freedom and happiness," Ron exhorts. "You need to decide in advance what kind of family you want to have and the values you want them to emulate. Then allow your purchases to line up with those values."

What does Proverbs 24:3-4 say about how to truly build your home and where true riches come from?

_____

_____

_____

_____

_____

Make your kids wait for what they want. We live in a society that seeks instant gratification: "Your way, right away!" "I want it all; I want it now!" But we know that's not how the Lord works. Cultivating trust and patience in your children ultimately cultivates character. And godly character is what kids need to get through this media-laden world victoriously. So teach them to wait and to save and to *pray* for what they want. Teach them that God ultimately is their provider, not you, not them and certainly not the world.

What do Psalm 34:10 and James 1:17 have to say about this?

_____

_____

_____

_____

Getting Creative

Plan a family game night, but not just any family game night—a group game night. Invite your covenant friends, the grandparents, those you want to reach out to, single adults from your church, etc.—not necessarily all of them, but a few others besides your immediate family. Have food and music and two or three fun games ready to play. Let the kids help pick out the games, plan the menu and decide who to invite. If they're old enough, maybe they can plan it all, but make sure that even the planning provides an opportunity for you to connect with them. Jot down some ideas here.

When will you have your family game night? _____

_____

What games do have at your house to play (or perhaps you can have your guests bring a favorite)?

_____
_____
_____
_____

What other ideas can you think of to make a night like this fun and meaningful?

_____
_____
_____
_____
_____

How will you make it an opportunity to bond with your child/children from beginning to end?

_____
_____
_____
_____
_____

15

TEACHING YOUR KIDS TO BE DREAMERS

Your kids were born to change the world. They were born to make a difference. Do they know that? Do *you* know that? What kind of dreams has God put in your heart for your children? What dreams are nestled deep in their hearts that you can draw out? Do you want them to rise to the 2 percent of society or remain in the 98 percent? God has a mission for you—*will you accept it?*

Think Outside the Box

As you consider how to develop your kids into dreamers, think outside the box and help *them* to think creatively and innovatively as well. Don't just do what other kids are doing, do something new, different, excellent—something a little *counter-culture*.

One thing Ron has encouraged his kids to do is to take odd jobs to earn money that they can then "donate . . . to help *other* people, not just satisfy their own purchasing power."

Do your children have any charities that they give to, or worthy causes they raise money for?

A great way to teach them about giving and helping others—while learning about other cultures—is to go online and search out various ministries to children around the world. They might decide to "adopt" a child in Uganda, pray for an orphanage in China, or give to supply Bibles to children in the Middle East. You can also read books and magazine articles together that deal with the cultures and/or needs of kids around the world. Doing this might set their hearts ablaze for missions or stir them with compassion for kids who have lost their parents to war or AIDS.

When will you plan to do something like this with your child/children? Write the date and time below:

_____

_____

Ron and Katie also teach their kids to *work* to be able to buy what they want. As we mentioned last chapter, this ties in directly to them learning how to save.

What do the following Scriptures teach about a strong work ethic, and how can we instill this in our children?

Proverbs 12:11

_____
_____
_____
_____
_____

Proverbs 14:23

_____
_____
_____
_____

Proverbs 21:25

_____
_____
_____
_____
_____

Show them how to take a vision from an idea stage to completion. Let that sink in for a minute. Many adults would probably like to be shown that! Imagine how empowering that would be for a young person.

Read again how Ron helped his daughter launch a website that reached out to preteen girls. "She saw this truth: 'If I have a dream, I can learn how to go about achieving it, and I can accomplish something,'" Ron shares. "Help your kids find opportunities to impact other people and not just indulge themselves."

What idea of your child's can you begin to champion *right now?*

_____
_____
_____
_____
_____

What practical steps will you take to help him or her take this idea out of his/her head and into reality?

_____
_____
_____
_____
_____
_____

As you do this, remember Ron's encouragement that we are always looking to plant seeds about being "others-centered."

Experiences that Inspire

Summer camp is fun, but what about a summertime experience in which your child learns to serve, sees another culture or hones a particular sport or skill? Even when they're young, get them thinking—and going places—outside the box, and give them experiences that inspire. Ron reminds us that "if MTV is going after kids at younger and younger ages, then so must we. We must plant in our kids a desire to really make a difference and change the world."

What kinds of activities and trips might you plan for your kids that will get "them out of their little comfort zone" this summer, at Christmas or spring break?

_____
_____
_____
_____
_____

What about throughout the year? On weekends?

_____

_____

_____

_____

_____

_____

Where are you in terms of your child going on a missions trip to another country? Would you say no right now, be okay with it, or get excited about it? Explain.

_____

_____

_____

_____

_____

_____

_____

Ponder Ron's words: "Letting our children have this experience is a test for us as parents, a test of our trust that God will take care of our kids. Allowing them to go out of the country sends our children a message while they are young that they were born for greatness and destined to impact the world!"

The Influence of Friends and Media

Do your kids' friends help them grow, or do they bring them down? What kind of influence are they having? Hopefully your children inspire others to greatness and have a heart for leading others to the Lord and to their dreams, but they have to be careful about who they spend the bulk of their time with.

You can influence the kinds of friends they have, and you have the authority to limit—or deny—their time with anyone. Make your home a "dream catcher"—think of it like a net for pulling in kids who will be a positive influence on your kids and for encouraging and shaping those who aren't so positive. Be one of those who call out the dreams of this *generation* and not just for your own kids.

Who do your kids spend the most time with (list here)?

_____
_____
_____
_____

What positive or negative impact are these friends having on your child/children?

_____
_____
_____
_____

Proverbs 12:26 says, "A righteous man is cautious in friendship, but the way of the wicked leads them astray." How can you teach your children to be cautious about who they choose to have as a close friend?

_____
_____
_____
_____
_____

Just as you don't want other kids stealing your kids' childlike heart to dream, so you don't want the media to do it either. "At the most, [media] can pour bad values into them," Ron writes. "At the very least, it preoccupies their mind so that they are not dreaming and thinking." Don't let the Machine steal their dreams or their time! Set boundaries and limits to what and how much they can consume. If they're out there dreaming and changing the world, they probably won't even notice!

Getting Creative

What incentives can you give for getting good grades, being creative, and demonstrating good character? Ron says, "Reward your kids with words, money, encouragement, opportunities, going out to do something fun together. If our value system is really about family values, and we really want them to be creative people, then let's reward the things we know are going to send our kids down that road."

He also advises us to share the stories of great men and women with them. Take them to the stories in the Bible that we've discussed, and point out to them how David, Daniel, Esther and Mary (to name a few) responded to the call of God in their youth and did amazing things in His power! Those are the kinds of movies you want to be watching, too, when you are having a family movie night—movies about people who helped end slavery, who stood up for what they believed in, who lost their lives fighting for the faith.

So what incentives will you give your children, and for which things?

_____
_____
_____
_____
_____
_____

How will you intercede for your kids to become (or *continue being*) dreamers and world changers? Write your prayer for them here:

_____
_____
_____
_____
_____
_____
_____
_____
_____
_____
_____
_____
_____

WEEK 4

16

ONE GENERATION AWAY FROM EXTINCTION

"All of us, as members of the Body of Christ, owe it to the younger generation to give them a fair chance at not just having faith, but thriving in their faith," Ron says. "We must create a place in our local churches where they are free to be passionate about God and they love coming for their growth and to get real answers to the questions they're asking about life."

Do Ron's words describe your church: a place where kids are "free to be passionate about God" and can find "real answers to the questions they're asking about life"? This is one of the burning questions of this chapter and the second half of our study. The question is not only, Is your church a place like this, but also, Is *the Church* in America a *people* that the younger generation wants to connect with?

Read Judges 2:10-12. What did the new generation "not know"?

_____

_____

_____

_____

What did this lack of knowledge and instruction lead to?

_____

_____

_____

_____

Why did their fathers—a generation who *clearly* saw the Spirit and power of God at work among them—fail to teach them adequately about the Lord and their own history?

_____

_____

_____

_____

What should the adult generation of believers in our nation be doing to prevent this from happening to our youth?

_____

_____

_____

_____

_____

What the Stats Tell Us

Ron says that, according to recent studies, only 5 percent of the next generation of Americans will be Bible-believing Christians. Weekly church attendance has dropped dramatically in the last 10 to 20 years. And it seems that thousands more churches close their doors each year than open them. What do we make of these statistics? What do they communicate to us and how should we respond? *What should we do?*

Why do you think this is the case in America today?

_____

_____

_____

_____

Where have we, as believers, gone wrong?

_____

_____

_____

_____

What must we do to turn these numbers around?

_____

_____

_____

_____

These numbers and the culture's increasing attitude of contempt for Christians and for things pertaining to God are no surprise to God Himself. What does 2 Peter 3:3-4 tell us about the last days?

_____

_____

_____

_____

Nonetheless, though the Word warns us that such will happen, we still have a responsibility to rescue our kids from hell and to woo their generation back to the heart of God.

Implications

What are some of the implications that Ron describes or that you see as a result of this downward spiral?

_____

_____

_____

_____

Ron writes, "By allowing our own young people to be submerged in culture, it's pulling them away from the things of God and dramatically impacting not just America but the entire world."

America—and all the pop culture we produce—has a profound impact on the world. When you think about raising up young dreamers, about making your sons and daughters sharp arrows for the Lord's use, think about this: Their dreams could impact an entire generation, an entire nation, *the entire world*. Britney Spears's dream has. Michael Jackson's did. J. K. Rowling's dreams (author of Harry Potter) are.

Ron says that MTV has established itself in 169 countries and 28 languages. Pastors from around the world call him and plead for help, saying that their kids have become more a part of "our" culture (or, rather, MTV's culture) than their own. But what about transferring them to *God's culture*? What would it take to win a generation around the world to Christ? What would it take to get the Word out as widely and as accessibly as MTV?

More Need = More Opportunity

Things might look gloomy, but we have to remember that the darker the darkness is, the brighter the light shines in contrast. As Romans 5:20 puts it, "Where sin increased, grace increased all the more." In other words, the greater the need for truth, love, genuineness and purity, the greater our opportunity to bring it. Ron says that the peak of this current generation is about 18 years old. Most Americans who come to Christ do so before age 20. "So there's a holy urgency," Ron says, "that we go after this generation before they enter their twenties."

How many young people do you know who are between the ages of 13 and 20 years old?

_____

_____

_____

_____

What kind of influence do you have on these young people (are they your kids' friends, your students, your church members, family members)?

_____

_____

_____

_____

Start getting the wheels of your mind turning now about how you can more deeply impact these young men and women. Right now would be a good time to stop and pray for them—and to pray for yourself, that you might have insight for reaching and inspiring them. Ron writes:

> There's an opportunity right now to reach out to young people and rescue them before they get into their 20s. Think of those who are on drugs in your community, the girls who are getting pregnant, the people who walk by you in a store with tattoos and piercings, and the ones who are looking for a family in a gang somewhere. These are the ones who need to be rescued. The kids in your church need to be deeply engaged in the things of God and equipped to stand against the culture.

The whole church itself must be willing to change and be moldable in order to take the tried and true message of the gospel to a younger generation. God's truth never changes. How we communicate can and should change to connect with a younger generation.

Have you thought about that? Changing your approach or your style of communicating the Truth for the benefit of a younger generation? That's what it's about, right? Not being content with the status quo, with hymns and church pews and a handful of people we've known for years—but having a holy *discontent* with the current state of this generation and a willingness to do what it takes to reach them. Remember, it's going to take *sacrifice*, sacrifice at home and at church and in the community.

Your Mission

Rather than end this chapter as we've ended the others, stop and take time right now to consider your mission. Ask God what He's equipping you to do with and for the youth of this generation. Let's join with Ron in saying, "We are going to be the ones that make it really hard for teenagers to go to hell in our town." Keeping kids out of hell often means engaging with hell itself.

Read Ephesians 6:18. What does this verse say to do?

_____

_____

_____

_____

Can you—are you willing to—stand in the gap for these young people? Will you commit to intercede for them and be "alert and always keep on praying" for them?

Now look at verse 19. Will you pray this over your pastor, youth pastor and over spiritual leaders and lay people alike who you see waging war with the enemy to rescue teenagers from hell?

This is your assignment. Will you accept it?

17

CREATING A CHURCH WHERE TEENS WANT TO COME

What's the scenario at your house before church on Sundays? Is church just part of the routine, something the family attends for two hours before heading to a more anticipated lunch? Are the kids dragging their heels (or worse) about going? *Or* is it something that you all wake up excited for, something that your kids look forward to? Do they get excited about worshiping God there and being with those people? Are they growing as a result? Ron writes, "Once kids do come to Christ, we've got to make sure they're involved in a church environment that actually feeds their faith and helps them grow." Is that happening at your church?

The Heart of a NextGen Church

In chapter 17, Ron introduces the "NextGen Church." He describes it as a haven, a refuge from the "hurricane crashing against the hearts and minds of this young generation." One essential element of an effective NextGen church is *relationships*—authentic, caring ones. "Once we have young people who begin to love God and want to follow His truth," Ron says, "we need to make sure they have a circle of friends and relationships that help inspire their faith." After all, for what reason are teens and young adults turning to things like MySpace and other online communities and chat rooms anyway? They're looking for a place to bond, a place to fit in, a place to be themselves.

Jesus actually prayed that we would be such a body. Read John 17:19-23. How many references to oneness or unity does He make in this passage? What does this—and His references to His relationship with His Father—indicate about the importance of our relationships?

_____

_____

_____

_____

As Ron starts taking us through imagining a church that young people are excited to be at, eager to worship God and hungry for the Word, does it reflect what you see in your church? If not, keep dreaming: "Imagine a place where they step out of the middle of the hammering storm, and a culture that is trying to destroy them, when they enter church. As soon as they walk in the door they say, 'Wow! I'm home. I'm on fire for God, and I feel normal being here!'" Imagine—it could begin with you!

And imagine that those who come in from the storm won't always be pretty, clean, well-mannered kids. They might have *messy* lives. Are you willing to deal with that? Not only to tolerate it, but to reach out to and *embrace* them? Are you eager to be part of the "clean-up" process (without giving them the feeling that they're dirty when they walk in the door)?

Ron says, "The first step in becoming a NextGen church is to examine our heart." What does 1 Corinthians 1:26-29 communicate about this?

_____

_____

_____

_____

_____

And what about the "first missionary" Jesus commissioned? Could a visitor to your church get much messier than the man we read about in Mark 5:1-13 and 18-20?

_____

_____

_____

_____

Rallying Around the Cause of Youth Ministry

Do adults embrace young people at your church? How are youth involved in Sunday services?

_____

_____

_____

_____

_____

Do young people sit in the front rows or run to the front for worship? Describe a typical worship service.

_____

_____

_____

_____

_____

_____

_____

"Kids know whether they are loved and accepted," Ron writes. "We can have a youth program and building with lights and sound for kids, but they know if the congregation considers them important." Are they important in your church and do they have a place beyond the youth group? When was the last time a young person got up in your church and gave a testimony? Have you noticed any teens attending church alone or with friends, but without their parents? Ron stresses the urgency and importance of not only being concerned with these kids, but of getting other people concerned, compassionate and *passionate* about their lives as well. We must be proactive.

What's something that you can do to help your church and other believers get on board in the mission to love and encourage teens?

_____

_____

_____

_____

Are the adults in your church rallying around the cause of youth ministry? If not, or if there seems to be some kind of disconnect, something lacking in this area, what can you and your spouse, your small group or your staff, if you're a pastor, do to become more focused on your young people?

_____

_____

_____

_____

_____

A Surpassing Subculture

The goal in creating a strong culture in the church, Ron says, is that *"teens feel more of a connection to your church and to your youth ministry than they feel to the world."* A church with a positive subculture becomes attractive to those outside of it and becomes a place where young people want to be. Creating a culture that "inspires, empowers and let's young people know that in a very deep way, you are committed to them," means creating a place where youth can flourish and grow into strong men and women.

What's the subculture of your church like? Do kids want to be there? Why or why not?

_____

_____

_____

_____

Does your church have a subculture that overpowers the culture at large? If so, why?

_____

_____

_____

_____

But, Ron is quick to point out, "The church doesn't try to compete with the world to be cool." Rather:

> Those who attend don't care what the culture of the world says, because they are so excited about the culture of the church that has changed their life. The ministry there continues to take place, and it keeps people coming back. It's life-giving, exciting, thrilling. It's adventurous.
>
> It's possible to live in a very stark secular society with a thriving subculture in a church that feeds individuals to a point where the church is not only existing, but it is growing in the midst of that secular society. As a result, adults and young people are thriving in their faith and becoming more like Jesus in spite of the downward pull of the secular culture.

"Shouldn't we work just as hard, if not harder, than companies like MTV to reach out and rescue our precious young people?" Ron asks. What is your vision for your church? What is your vision for your children? What is your hope for the youth in your city? It's time to strive for more. "Good enough" is not good enough anymore. We serve an amazing God who has an amazing dream for this generation. Won't you grab hold of it?

Getting Creative

As noted previously, we won't go too far without prayer. Our good ideas, without God, won't go far. But with Him, all things are possible, and in His strength we can do great things. Will you consider calling a prayer meeting to gather people together to seek God for the youth of your church and your city? If so, when and where will you do this?

A Project

What's important to the teens in your church? Why not take the time to find out?

Ron says that we need "to make children a part of church life while they are young, and address issues that are important to them from the Bible. We need to get young people to embrace what happens on Sunday mornings. We need to make sure that what goes on at church is feeding their souls. We need to make sure that we as pastors and preachers are speaking into *a young person's life and heart* (not speaking just to the adults)."

If we want to know what's relatable to them, we have to do the research. There are many ways to do this. You can create a survey of a few questions to ask the teens, or a certain number of teens, in your church. Or gather a group of teens together for a meeting to discuss what they want to hear and how they want to be involved. Or you can just start talking with kids over the course of the next couple months. Talk to your own! However you do it, you must make the effort to *listen*. Then make the commitment to act on what you hear.

18

DREAMERS FOR GOD

Where are the old men who dream dreams? Where are the old women who dream dreams? Ron opens this chapter talking about believing adults—be they 30, 60 or 85—dreaming dreams for the younger generation. He points out how Joel 2:28 says, "your old men will dream dreams." It's time for you to ask God to pour out His Spirit on *you* and on a generation of dreamers who need to be reawakened!

They Didn't Ask for this Garbage

It took "old men"—or *dirty old men,* rather—dreaming up the destructive TV shows, movies, music and magazines that ensnare kids today; it will take our dreaming holy dreams to take back what their nightmares have stolen. Producers of pop culture and media are "preying on our young people because young people have lots of money to spend," Ron warns. "They appeal to young people's most base desires to get them to spend their money. But the fact is, the kids didn't ask for this garbage; they were sold this garbage by people trying to make a lot of money."

And, really, it's an older, perverse generation playing on *their own* base desires. And they don't care who gets dumped on in the process. Actually they do care—they care that they make money doing it. And so, they make what can never satisfy look cool to kids; they market that which carves a hole in the heart, which they then attempt to fill with more idolatry and self-indulgence. It's a vicious, downward cycle.

How do you see today's media and pop culture producers reflected in Romans 1:28-31?

_____

_____

_____

In Philippians 2:15-16, Paul writes that he wants you to "become blameless and pure, children of God without fault in a crooked and depraved generation, in which you shine like stars in the universe as you hold out the word of life." Don't you want your children standing out like stars in the universe, holding out the *word of life* to the world? Do you have a dream to see the kids in your city "become blameless and pure, children of God without fault in a crooked and depraved generation"? Then *that's* what we must become first!

How can we purify our own hearts in order to receive the dreams God has for us? One way is found in Romans 12:2. What is that way?

_____

_____

_____

_____

How can our young people keep their hearts pure and prepared to be vessels of God's dreams? (See Psalm 119:1-16.)

_____

_____

_____

Dreamers for God

Ron asks, "I wonder: *If God really does want to touch and rescue this young generation, is He waiting for the older men, all the adults and the moms and the dads to dream on behalf of the young people?*"

Psalm 110:3 says, "Your people will volunteer freely in the day of Your power; in holy array, from the womb of the dawn, your youth are to You as the dew" (*NASB*). *Today* is the day of the Lord's power! Are you "volunteering freely"? Are you giving of your life to help array this young generation in holiness?

Take a moment to reflect on the following from chapter 18:

What would it be like to have 100 kids, 500 kids, 1,000 kids in our church youth groups? What would it be like to have an incredible worship team for Wednesday night services where our kids are smitten with love for God? What would it take to have buses that pick up kids who can't find rides to church on

Sunday mornings and Wednesday nights? . . . *Where are the dreamers?* If we don't dream like that, the youth won't come.

How do you feel when you read this?

_____

_____

_____

_____

What will you dare to dream? How big, how high, how wide are you willing to expand your imagination, and how much are you willing to trust God Almighty for?

_____

_____

_____

_____

Without taking time to ponder it, write down *three big dreams* just as Ron has written in the paragraph above. Write them just like he did, as questions (e.g., *What would it take to birth a youth center out of our church? What would it take to get kids off the streets in our city?*)

1. _____

_____

2. _____

_____

3. _____

_____

In what ways is your church a "dream center" for kids?

_____

_____

_____

In what ways would you like it to be?

_____

_____

_____

_____

What would it take to gather in "the strays" of your community—those kids being raised without God and/or without the love of a great family? Jot down some ideas.

_____

_____

_____

_____

What If?

Ron says, "A dreamer is someone who asks, 'What if?'" We can't be afraid to dream! Too many people let self-doubt and pessimism stop them before they even give *God* a chance to start! What does it cost you to dream? That's what is so beautiful, and so fun, about dreaming—it costs us nothing! Ron exhorts us to start asking "WHAT IF . . .?"

Think about the young dreamers in the Bible that we've already talked about: David, Daniel, Mary, Esther. And then there's Joseph in Genesis, and the young Kings Solomon and Josiah, and Mark and Timothy in the New Testament. What if they had *doubted* the dreams God gave them and refused to follow through, afraid of the outcome? Perhaps the Jews would have been annihilated; the Temple never built; Jesus not born; or God would have found others to take the place of those dreamers. Would you want to lose your shot at something so great? They all faced extraordinary circumstances, and yet they trusted the God of the impossible, the God that they knew could accomplish extraordinary miracles through them.

Read Daniel 3:8-30. What do you think were the "what ifs" going through these young men's minds when they refused to bow before Nebuchadnezzar?

_____

_____

_____

What were the results of their trusting in God rather than bowing to fear?

_____

_____

_____

_____

What would have happened had they refused to dream?

_____

_____

_____

Ron asks the following questions that are worth revisiting and writing answers to here. Write a few sentences for each of the following:

What if God wants to just pour out His spirit on countless young people? What would it take? What would we have to do to be ready for that as a church? As an individual?

_____

_____

_____

What if He wants to use your church to be a center for rescuing a generation? Once they came, what would you do with them? How would your church disciple them? How would your church train them to be leaders?

_____

_____

_____

How do we train kids to disciple other kids?

_____

_____

_____

God's Heart for You

We often hear the phrase, "God loves you and has a plan for your life." Indeed, He does; but that plan is part of a much bigger plan to win the human race to Himself and spread His love to the world. While He loves each one of us deeply and passionately, He wants that love to translate into our loving other people and getting caught up in His grand master plan. Pause now and ask God to show you how you fit into this grand plan. What is *your* role? Do you know how important your part is? Never underestimate how He can use you—your prayers, your hands, your words, your *dreams*—to bring glory to His name and salvation to a desperate generation.

19

ANATOMY OF A NEXTGEN CHURCH

Ron reminds us that the mission of the Church since the beginning has been to pass on the faith to our children and to entire generations after us. In Exodus 10:2, the Lord says, "That you may tell your children and grandchildren . . . how I performed my signs among them, and that you may know that I am the LORD." And Psalm 22:30-31 tells us, "Posterity will serve him; future generations will be told about the Lord. They will proclaim his righteousness to a people yet unborn—for he has done it." The psalmist was already thinking about a generation yet to be born. How much more should we be pondering and planning to reach the young ones now living on Earth?

Following are four key ingredients of a NextGen church, followed by a study of those serving as examples. As you read this chapter in *Re-Create* and in this workbook, keep a separate notebook handy. Jot down your thoughts and what stands out to you in it. Make it your "NextGen" journal, something you can refer to again and again and can use to chronicle your dreams and prayers for your children, your church and this generation.

Ingredient #1: Urgency

Mobilize the troops! This is WAR! We must sound the battle cry to the church and enlist *everyone* in the service of saving young people. The devil has declared war on this generation, and he's using weapons of mass destruction to take them out. Those weapons are launched via the TV, computer, Xbox, stereo and teen magazine, among others. He has sought to destroy generations throughout history, sometimes through outright murder, as we see in Exodus 1–2 and Matthew 2 (and as he's doing today with abortion), and sometimes through craftier means.

Ron says that "in a NextGen church, the entire congregation understands the urgency of reaching this generation." They recognize that there is no time to lose and there is no one too young or insignificant to rescue.

What specifically can you do *this week* or this month to help mobilize your congregation?

_____

_____

_____

What information or resources do you think your church is lacking in this department? What can you do to get those to them?

_____

_____

_____

_____

Not feeling the urgency yet? Take five minutes to meditate on the following verse: "Deliver those who are being taken away to death and those who are staggering to slaughter, *Oh hold them back!*" (Proverbs 24:11, *NASB*; emphasis added).

Ingredient #2: An Aggressive Plan to Grow the Youth Ministry

What's your (or your church's) strategy to double the size of your youth group? What are you doing as a church to draw your city's youth through the church doors and into your homes and lives?

In what area of this mission do you find yourself most qualified (not that you *have* to be qualified—the Bible is replete with stories of God using the least qualified people to do the most extraordinary things)? Or, maybe better put, in what areas are you *gifted* and *passionate*? Perhaps you're a dancer or a choreographer who can help kids create a team that uses dance, sports and the arts to reach out to their peers. Or maybe you're a businessman who has money and expertise to share and a heart for mentoring young visionaries.

How are you personally coaching your kids to witness to others and to cry out to and for this generation?

_____

_____

_____

_____

It's not about numbers for numbers' sake, for saying that you have a 5,000-member congregation. It's about numbers for *salvation*, numbers of transformed lives and numbers of young people snatched out of the lion's (Satan's) mouth. It's about striking back at a world that's stealing our youth and selling them to sexual exploitation, self-absorption, drug use, satanism and suicide.

Ingredient #3: All-Church Involvement

"The next step is to constantly cast the vision and invite people in the congregation to get involved in the plan to double and disciple," Ron says. "Mentors are needed." Do you have a "Timothy" or two (or twelve!) in your life—someone you are mentoring, discipling and being a friend to? Someone you're allowing to walk with you and watch your life?

If you are mentoring someone, do you meet with that person once a week for coffee or do you allow him or her to connect with you regularly and to simply watch how you live? Are you getting into the Word with him or her and into the deep things of the heart? Are you really *training* that individual to be a mature Christian? If not, how can you begin to do that?

_____

_____

_____

_____

_____

How can you inspire the seniors of your spiritual family to come on board and take their places as warriors and dreamers for this generation?

_____

_____

_____

_____

_____

Name three people age 70 or older that you can recruit *today*:

1. _____

2. _____

3. _____

Ingredient #4: Sunday Services Reflecting a Heart for Youth

Does your church reflect a genuine heart of love for kids and teens? Do you see *tangible evidence* of that each and every Sunday, such as older adults engaging young people in conversation, your kids' friends being welcomed with warmth and sincerity, hugs and affirmation given to teens, leaders alert for those in need of prayer? Do the grandparents of your congregation "have the joy of seeing young people worshiping with all their heart"? And do "they have the confidence of knowing that they are putting the baton firmly in the next generation's hand"?

We have to be willing to give up our preferences. "A certain style is not what is holy. The Word of God is holy. The truth is holy," Ron exhorts. "Making God's truth relatable to a young generation is the highest level of virtue that we could possibly live in making the gospel accessible to the next generation."

Is your Sunday service "about engaging young people through the music and the message and involving them in the actual service itself"?

_____

_____

_____

Are there any stylistic preferences that *you* are hanging on to that you need to sacrifice for the greater good? What specifically?

_____

_____

_____

Examples

Reading the examples of Hillsong Church, Prestonwood Baptist Church, New Life Church, Bethany World Outreach Center, Fellowship Church, The City Church and others, what do you glean from them that you can bring into your own church life?

_____

_____

_____

_____

How do their stories inspire you in your quest to reach the youth of this generation?

_____

_____

_____

_____

_____

_____

_____

Getting Creative

Remember Ron's words: "Becoming a NextGen church is not a far-fetched dream . . . it's going to take a lot of us working together, but we can do this. It is so fulfilling when your church has become a hospital for a brokenhearted generation and is full of life, passion and determination to rescue kids. If you focus on young people and show them that you love them, they will respond. They will come to Christ. When they know that they are wanted and valued, they will gladly engage deeply in becoming a member of the kingdom of God that takes the message of Christ into the future, to the whole world."

Your project this week? Keep working on your NextGen journal in which you write your reflections, questions, prayers, plans and _dreams_ for your children, your church and the youth of your city (and beyond!). Let it be something that you keep and use beyond this study. Take it with you in your car, to work, to church. Record your observations. What are you seeing in the youth culture around you? What is the Holy Spirit whispering to you in the quietness of your heart? Be creative with it—put magazine clippings, quotes and drawings of ideas in it. The sky's the limit! Remember, _you're a dreamer,_ and dreamers put their dreams on paper in order to later write them into reality!

CHURCHES THAT BREAK THE MOLD: DOUBLE VISION STORIES

But I'm Not Even a Pastor; What Can I Do?

You are an advocate. You're a man or a woman whose heart has been stirred to rescue a generation. You're someone whose time, talent, expertise and love are invaluable to the youth you can reach. You're like a secret weapon in the Warrior's hand. While the enemy has his eye on the youth pastor and the youth group, targeting them for attack, you can come in from behind, interceding, interacting and influencing your church and the kids in it. Don't give in to the lie that you have nothing to give—you have a lot more than you might think.

Read Exodus 1:15-21. How were these midwives *advocates* for the baby boys that Pharaoh wanted to kill?

_____

_____

_____

In what ways can you be a "spiritual midwife" for youth in your church and in your city?

_____

_____

_____

Ron writes, "Many of these NextGen churches started with an advocate just like you. You can become a champion for the young people in your church and in your community. Go to your youth pastor and say, 'I'm here for you. I want you to know that I want to do everything I can to help your ministry to these kids and rescue this generation.'" Can you do that? Can you go to your pastor or youth pastor and say just that? As an advocate, you're an influencer. You can influence the youth pastor with the things God has impressed upon your heart. And you have a sphere of influence that extends to people he couldn't reach. Think of all the people you know!

What is one way you can *advocate* for the kids in your church?

_____

_____

_____

For the kids in your city?

_____

_____

_____

For kids in America and/or worldwide?

_____

_____

_____

Make a list of all the people with whom you have a relationship and can influence to labor for the youth of our nation (write small or get a big piece of paper, because it's going to be a long list!):

_____

_____

_____

_____

_____

Make another list of people with whom you think you are influential, but you don't actually know (could be an acquaintance, friend of a friend, or a total stranger you want to get to know and could influence):

_____

_____

_____

_____

_____

Now, go back over your lists and jot down notes next to each person's name about *how* you can influence them. As Ron says, "Its one thing for you to share with people; it's another for them to be deeply informed." Perhaps you can begin a Bible study, book club or discussion group in which you talk about the youth in your community and how you can bring about change in the youth culture and bring those kids to Christ. You could keep it within your church or aim for citywide church involvement. Or perhaps you could plan a rally in which concerned Christians in your community come together to get informed and inspired.

Another Advocate

Merriam-Webster's Collegiate Dictionary defines "advocate" as (1): one that pleads the cause of another, (2): one that defends or maintains a cause or proposal and (3): one that supports or promotes the interests of another. There is someone you should be well acquainted with who is all of those things for you. He is Jesus. First John 2:1 says that "we have one who speaks to the Father in our defense—Jesus Christ, the Righteous One." He pleads your cause to the Father; He defends you; He promotes and encourages you.

How can you support and promote that which is in the very best interest of the young people around you, even if you don't know them personally? How can you defend them?

_____

_____

_____

_____

_____

One way you can plead for them is to *intercede* for them (by the way, an advocate is also considered an *intercessor*). Maybe you're already praying daily for this generation or the youth of your church and/or city. But if you're not, pick one day out of the week in which you will specifically focus your prayer time on interceding for them.

What day and time will it be? _____

_____

Who will you ask to join you (whether in person, on the phone or in spirit) during this time?

_____

_____

_____

_____

Provoked by Passion—God's Heart for You

Your Advocate, Jesus, was provoked by passion for you enough to die on the cross. Will you allow your passion to rescue young people to provoke you to make sacrifices as well? Will you become so passionate about youth and seeing them saved and set free that you provoke yourself and others around you to action? Commit your passion and your dedication to action to Jesus right now.

Write your prayer and your commitment here:

_____

_____

_____

_____

_____

_____

_____

_____

Remember Ron's encouragement: "Our job, as members of the kingdom of God, is to go after these kids *more passionately than the world is going after them*. As an advocate, you can provoke that passion and help create a culture in your church that is more powerful than the culture in the world. In this way, once a kid is committed to Christ, he finds his long-lost family—the place where he belongs, the place he can't wait to come back to. As a result, he and others like him are protected from the garbage of the world and are set up to become the champions who will influence their generation for Christ."

21

DREAMERS ALWAYS WIN (THE CULTURE WAR)

Ron says that the dreams of pop culture and media manufacturers compel the hearts and minds of the young people in our communities and in our families: "The current shapers of culture have successfully dreamed a dream and then wooed the lion's share of the young generation to march to the beat." The challenge before us now is: *Can we create a culture that causes kids to move to the beat of a different drum?*

One of the reasons why kids, and people in general, fall prey to the pull of pop culture is for the fantasy it offers—a fantasy of a life of leisure, of being the center of attention, of endless sexual pleasure, of power and control, and of having whatever you want whenever you want it. People "escape" to that world, subconsciously searching for freedom from their *real* lives. And the media's right there to help them. As we discussed earlier, 2 Peter 2:19 describes it accurately: "They promise them freedom, while they themselves are slaves of depravity—for a man is a slave to whatever has mastered him." But the Bible speaks of a different kind of freedom.

Read 2 Corinthians 3:17, James 1:25 and Galatians 5:1. According to these verses, from where (or from whom) does true freedom come?

_____

_____

_____

_____

How can we help young people find and live in this freedom?

_____

_____

_____

_____

A Seemingly Impossible Task

So who or what is dominating American culture right now? Who's winning the culture war—and the war for the hearts of our youth? Turn on your car radio and peruse the channels—what do you hear? What about on TV and on magazine racks? Those who are winning the culture war, Ron says, have "done it by dreaming big and incorporating young people into their dream."

So now we must dream dreams big enough to transform our families, churches, communities and the culture at large. Sound overwhelming? It is—and it should be. If it wasn't, we wouldn't depend fully on God to make it happen. But when we depend on Him fully, then we will give Him the glory fully, when we see the impossible come to pass.

If you feel like a small fish in a very large pond, wondering what kind of difference you can possibly make, go to the Word. The Bible is filled with stories of the extraordinary. Actually, little that we read of there is very "ordinary" at all. And many of the heroes of the faith that we read about started out simply as small fish in big ponds to whom God gave big dreams and impossible tasks!

One young dreamer was Joseph. After being sold by his brothers into slavery, then put into jail over a false accusation and remaining there for years, Joseph got summoned by Pharaoh to interpret a dream. God revealed the meaning of Pharaoh's dream to Joseph and Joseph revealed it to Pharaoh.

Read Genesis 41:28-41. What does Joseph advise Pharaoh to do to keep Egypt alive throughout the predicted famine?

_____

_____

_____

_____

What is Pharaoh's response to Joseph?

_____

_____

_____

_____

How does Joseph then suddenly have tremendous influence over the entire nation of Egypt and beyond?

_____

_____

_____

Joseph was an interpreter of dreams and one to whom God gave vivid dreams in his sleep, but do you think he also had to be a "dreamer" in the sense that we've been discussing in order to accomplish the task set before him? How so?

_____

_____

_____

_____

What do you believe God could possibly do with *your* life to impact your entire city? The culture at large?

_____

_____

_____

_____

"So where do I start?" you might be asking. The good news is that you've already started! Sitting here, right now, reading this book and doing this study is the first step to being proactive about making change. Next, if you haven't started already, start to *dream*. Start writing down those dreams, brainstorming more dreams, discussing your dreams with like-minded people, and discussing your kids' dreams with them. Ron says, "We need to dream a big dream of the part of the culture we want to affect and then roll up our sleeves."

When you read his example of Rudy Giuliani in New York City—*with one signature he shut down thousands of triple-X porn distribution centers!*—does it inspire you to think on a grander scale? Why or why not?

_____

_____

_____

_____

What comes to mind that you could do to bring about such transformation of your own city?

_____

_____

_____

Your Dream Is Your Voice

If we want to bring this kind of change to our culture, our city and our nation, "we can't just come with problems; we have to come with solutions," Ron admonishes.

What are one or two things in your community, city, your culture or country that you often complain about and/or point the finger at?

_____

_____

_____

_____

What solution (or beginnings of a solution) can you think of for that problem? Write down a few thoughts.

_____

_____

_____

_____

Ron talks about dreaming dreams for the kids we see on the streets or those who are on drugs or who are having babies in high school. Get a vision for them! Ask God to give you His heart and His wisdom for reaching them and turning their situation into our (and ultimately, their) opportunity!

Think of the impact you could have on the kids in your community not by merely telling them not to vandalize or not to skateboard here or there, but by affirming them and *inspiring* them to take their dreams and talents to another level—by calling them *up* to a higher level of living!

"*People follow dreams not directives,*" Ron says. "They won't do what they are told to do or what they are supposed to do. But they will do what they are inspired to do."

Getting Creative

"So now it's time to dream a dream for the kids you don't know," Ron says, "the kids who aren't in your family, the kids you may never meet." He says that it is our responsibility "to shield them from our present culture's heinous belief system" and that "we must exercise our influence to protect them." What teens do you know of who don't have parents operating proactively in their lives (or don't have parents, period)? We are called as believers to step in, to dream dreams and to do battle on their behalf.

Think of kids in your community who are in need. It could be your son's or daughter's friend who you know has a horrible home life. It could be the group of pierced, tattooed punk rockers smoking pot in the park. It could be gangsters or loners or pregnant teen girls you see around town. What could be your first step in reaching out to them?

_____

_____

_____

_____

How could you find a way to find out their story? How could you get informed so that you might better understand and therefore better minister to them?

_____

_____

_____

_____

What step will you take *this week* to go about doing that?

_____

_____

_____

How will you apply Daniel 12:3 to your dreams for these kids and for the culture at large?

_____

_____

_____

_____

WEEK 5

22

PARALYZED BY THE ORDINARY

Ron writes, "I wonder if we have been so programmed by what we call 'normal American culture' that we think we're supposed to find a way to just survive in the midst of it rather then be a change agent in it?"

Read that again.

Have we become so paralyzed by the normal and by wanting to be "tolerant" that we've abdicated our place as change agents? Or have we just never fully known the position of authority we have in Christ to expand His kingdom—and kingdom culture—on Earth?

Rethinking the Ordinary; Rediscovering Our Authority

What do the following passages communicate about our right and responsibility to bring Kingdom culture to the earth?

Matthew 6:9-10

_____
_____
_____
_____

Matthew 5:13-16

_____
_____
_____
_____

Psalm 8:4-6

_____
_____
_____

How do you translate being "salt and light" to the young people in your life?

_____

_____

_____

_____

What do Matthew 17:20 and 18:18 tell you about the *authority* you have in Christ to bring Kingdom culture to Earth (and to accomplish that which seems impossible)?

_____

_____

_____

_____

Pick an area of the culture that you'd like to begin praying for. Commit to pray every day for the next two weeks: "Lord, let Your kingdom come and Your will be done in _____ [Hollywood, the music industry, my child's school, our downtown area—you fill in the blank] as it is in heaven." Note here any changes you see or anything the Holy Spirit speaks to your heart about this area over the next couple weeks. Share what you see and hear with your spouse, small group or prayer partner.

"We look at the ordinary as the way things are *supposed to be*," Ron points out. Have you noticed yourself sliding into the status quo? Just going along with what the world says normal should be?

Our society is fixated on so-called "tolerance" and "political correctness." Under the premise of not offending or demeaning another person, even saying "Merry Christmas!" has all but become a crime. Reading stories about a mommy and a daddy (as opposed to a mommy and a mommy or a daddy and a daddy) is being considered discriminatory in some schools.

Do you fear the reprimands of the world in regard to this or are you fearless in your faith and in challenging the unrighteousness that's fast becoming "normal"? Reflect on that and answer honestly.

_____

_____

_____

_____

What does Proverbs 29:25 say about fearing man? What about trusting God?

_____

_____

_____

_____

_____

Effects of Living in the Ordinary

Ron says that when we compare ourselves with others in the "98 percent," it becomes all too easy to legitimize ordinariness and justify compromise in our lives. It's too easy to say, "Well, this is what everybody else is doing, so . . ." And we fear ruffling anyone else's feathers (but remember what Proverbs 29:25 says!). Fear, excuses, apathy, compromise are all effects of living in the ordinary. And that leads to a lackluster life. But Jesus says we are to be _LIGHT_ to the world! His desire for us is to shine like stars in the darkness of our culture! Ron says that another result of abiding in the ordinary is that we lose our idealism. He writes, "We are not supposed to live like _mere men_, like everybody else."

In what ways or what areas might you honestly say you've lost your idealism?

_____

_____

_____

_____

_____

_____

When we compare ourselves with the ordinary and decide we're okay with it, the impact on our life is minimized. But Ron points out the danger of such complacency. It's not just a matter of us not stepping out to dream or do great things; it's about the evil we let slip in _on our watch_. He says:

> If we see something happen that is horrible, we try to justify our lack of involvement. We're quick to point out the people who are putting horrible things in movies or on TV screens, _yet we do not do anything._

Ruffle Some Feathers!

Aren't you tired of being overrun by the ordinary? Of letting the bullies of "tolerance" and secularism bowl you over? Are you ready to rip the hand of complacency off your mouth and SPEAK OUT for what's right and stand up for those who have no voice yet?

What do the following Scriptures exhort us to do?

Proverbs 31:8-9

_____

_____

_____

_____

Proverbs 24:11-12

_____

_____

_____

_____

Ron challenges us, "We have to deal with the fact that the people who are destroying our kids do so on _our watch._ They are doing so _while we watch._ They did so while _we allowed it to happen,_ even if we may not have caused it. We allowed porn to come online. We didn't scream loud enough, and it became tolerated in our society."

Do you agree?

God's Heart for You

God's heart for you is as Jesus said: to be the salt of the earth and the light of the world. He has no desire to hide you—or for you to hide yourself—under a basket, or under the cloak of normalcy. He loves you too much to let you be normal and ordinary! Christians are called to be changers, to shake up the status quo. Christians are called to be martyrs, not just in the sense that we'll die for our faith, but that we'll die to ourselves and to our culture and our need to be approved of by the world. Many believers around the globe are persecuted and are dying for being bold enough to resist their culture's status quo.

Are you ready to rise up and join them? Are you ready to be radical in your devotion to God and your desire to see a generation transformed? If so, now is the time. If so, take 10, 20, 30 minutes or an hour to get on your knees before the Lord and repent for being paralyzed by the ordinary and for not speaking out against the evil things that people have tried to "normalize" in our culture. Then ask Him to spoil you for the ordinary! Ask Him to give you a *voice* and to help you act on what He shows you.

Take the challenge a step further: plan a time to fast (a day, three days, a week?) with your small group, your spouse, or with the entire church. Have a time of corporate prayer in which you bring all these things before the Lord, repent before one another and be encouraged by the Spirit and the Word. *This* is where change begins. This is where we shake off the ordinary and rise up to the high calling we have in Christ!

23

WINNING THE PR WAR

How do you react to what Ron describes early in chapter 23—the scene on the steps of San Francisco's city hall?

_____

_____

_____

_____

If you were a teen participating in that BattleCry Rally, how would feel being shouted at by the protestors?

_____

_____

_____

_____

What story in the Bible might this remind you of? Read Genesis 19:1-10.

_____

_____

_____

_____

Ron writes, "You would have been so proud of our young people. Their response was just to pray and be kind and loving, while singing worship songs. The media, of course, showed up because they love a catfight. But they saw how these kids were so loving and how the very people who were protesting and saying, 'This is a mean-spirited Christianity thing' were the ones who were yelling and angry."

Do you get excited when you read this? Does it inspire you to jump in and support this generation of young believers in taking their stance against the status quo of society?

What does Jesus say about us when we receive that kind of treatment and don't retaliate with angry words of our own? He says, "Blessed are those who are persecuted because of righteousness, for theirs is the kingdom of heaven. Blessed are you when people insult you, persecute you and falsely say all kinds of evil against you because of me. Rejoice and be glad, because great is your reward in heaven, for in the same way they persecuted the prophets who were before you" (Matthew 5:10-12). Ron goes on to say:

> It was shocking to see how violently opposed the protestors were to young people who just wanted to stand up for purity. As I reflect on it, I wonder why it is that the ultra-liberal people in San Francisco were so tolerant of every other group except Christians. It dawned on me that they don't mind if we keep our Christianity in our little youth group or in our church basement, as long as it stays inside four walls. But they really don't want us to bring it out into the public sector; they don't want us to bring it to the city hall or to the front steps of the courthouse. They don't want us to bring it up in politics or in the discussion of the values of our nation. Why? Because *they have virtually dominated our thinking and culture unopposed for so many years*. It angers them to see someone make a visible stand.

The PR War

How does biased reporting—reporting with a bent toward unbelievers—shape the way our culture views Christians and Christianity?

_____

_____

_____

_____

Have you seen any examples of this in your own city or even in your life? If so, what did they make Christians—or you—out to be?

_____

_____

_____

_____

Ron says, "To the mass population, perception is reality." How do you think the media has distorted people's perceptions in describing and defining Christians?

_____

_____

_____

_____

_____

What does Ron say we need to *over-communicate* in order to change that perception and bias in our culture?

_____

_____

_____

_____

What does Jesus say His people will be known by (see John 13:34-35)?

_____

_____

_____

_____

"As we meet people who are not Christians," Ron says, "we've got to overwhelm with God's love. As we talk about any of these issues, we need to talk about love. In fact, we need to display the kind of love and warmth that's real and genuine, and not just focus on debating ideas. We are battling for the hearts and souls of people, no matter what persuasion they might be." When it comes to the battle of ideas, we can meditate on 1 Corinthians 8:1, which says, "Knowledge puffs up, but love builds up."

Think of specific ways in which you can build people up through love, rather than puff yourself up by spouting knowledge, and write them here:

_____

_____

_____

_____

_____

Who in your sphere of influence (work, your child's school, your neighborhood, etc.) do you find most difficult to love? Is it someone who opposes your faith and your values?

_____

_____

_____

_____

How can you love that person genuinely while still acknowledging the differences between you?

_____

_____

_____

_____

How Is the PR War Won?

What are the four major arenas in which culture is influenced?

_____

_____

_____

_____

In what ways have you seen the world's value system invade two or more of these areas? Cite specific examples, stories, mindsets, rules or encounters.

_____

_____

_____

_____

_____

How have homosexuals specifically "normalized themselves" into our culture? How are they specifically targeting children and teens?

_____

_____

_____

_____

What does Ron cite as the reason homosexuals have had so much success in winning the PR war?

_____
_____
_____
_____

What is *your* plan for winning it back? Discuss with your group or your spouse, or simply write your thoughts here.

_____
_____
_____
_____

Ron reminds us that "we should sympathize with homosexuals because they are hurting and confused, but not for the reasons the activists espouse. . . . Again," he says, "let me emphasize, there is *no* good reason to persecute anyone for a sin if they are not believers."

Love is to be our aim. And, yet, we're still in a battle. It's a battle with spiritual principalities and powers, but also a battle to make our voice heard in a perverse culture and a battle to win the souls of the lost—young and old—before it's too late.

Getting Creative

Having a plan in place keeps us on track and accountable, much like having a budget on paper or on a computer program keeps us from overspending and helps us to save.

What part of the culture are you most passionate about changing? In which area do you think you could be most influential (identify as a starting point)? What would it take to see God's kingdom come and His will done in that area?

_____
_____
_____
_____
_____

Together with your spouse, prayer partner or small group, pray for that specific arena. (And if you don't have one in mind yet, ask God to put one on your heart.) Then begin to map out a plan for how you can bring *truth* and *light* and *transformation* to this area.

What do you dream it will look like in 10 years?

_____

_____

_____

_____

What practical steps can you take to start the process of change?

_____

_____

_____

_____

When will you do these things?

_____

_____

_____

Who can you talk to, minister with, form relationships with to become more influential in this area?

_____

_____

_____

_____

Write any other pertinent thoughts into your plan.

_____

_____

_____

_____

_____

Print it out and put it somewhere you'll see it. Keep dialoguing with others and praying about it.

24

WHO TOLD US TO SHUT UP?

The world around us is loud with people who are taking advantage of their right to free speech by spewing messages of immorality all over our kids and throughout the culture. The gay agenda, the abortion activists, the hip-hop icons and the plethora of Wiccans, Buddhists, yogis and atheists that war against godly values have all raised their voices of influence in our nation. And in the name of tolerance, they're all allowed equal airtime.

But what about Christians? What about believers raising their voices with the message of faith, hope and love? What about *our* right to freedom of speech?

The devil and the world seek to silence us, to brand us bigots for promoting godly values and promoting God Himself. But they are not entirely to blame. No, too many Christians in this country have bowed to the fear of man and the lie that we should be seen and not heard. It's time to shake out of that stupor, time to reject the fear of man and be bold to speak out in the name of Jesus.

Uninhibited Expressions of Faith

Many grand and beautiful things throughout the ages have been built, painted, played and performed to the glory of God. Many a martyr died in the Early Church, and many die today in other nations as they boldly proclaim the gospel and the truths pertaining to God. Unabashedly bold. Ron states:

> From the very beginning, Christianity has been a very vocal and public expression. In the Early Church, when people committed their lives to Christ, they confessed their belief in Christ in front of the masses and, as a result, many were killed . . . for it.

Have you ever been persecuted for sharing your faith, or shot down for voicing your moral or spiritual perspective? Describe such a time.

_____

_____

_____

_____

_____

_____

What makes you bashful about sharing your faith? Why?

_____

_____

_____

_____

_____

What does Jesus say to this in Mark 8:38?

_____

_____

_____

_____

Ron writes, "Much of the art renaissance that happened all across Europe in the 1500s was an expression of the artists' faith in Christ. When you look at masterpieces that Michelangelo produced and the amazing works of music that Handel composed, you can see that these people weren't shy and inhibited, afraid to express themselves. These were people who had the outflow of what was on the inside of them shaping their artwork for all to see."

Is your faith expressed in everything you do? How do you have the outflowing of what's on the inside of you shaping your work and life?

_____

_____

_____

_____

_____

Wherein can you make your greatest expression of faith? What's the gift or talent or passion in which you can be most bold?

_____

_____

_____

_____

Get Vocal About It

"We've been told in no uncertain terms that you are to be seen and not heard as Christians," Ron notes. But we don't have to be that. In contrast, what does God tell us we are to be?

How do the following verses speak to your heart in this area?

Proverbs 28:1

_____

_____

_____

Jeremiah 1:6-7

_____

_____

_____

Matthew 28:18-20

_____

_____

_____

2 Timothy 1:7

_____

_____

_____

And we have to ask, Are we really loving others when we remain silent? No. Sometimes the truth hurts to hear, but the truth is also what brings healing. To be silent might appease ungodly people for a moment, but it will harm them in the long run. We have to speak up for their sake and for the sake of the younger generation. We have to take our position in the battle for their hearts.

"In the culture war, whoever speaks up most gets to shape the culture," Ron says. "If we don't speak up, we lose. We speak with our vote, with our creativity, with our noticing when there are hints of unbiblical values being displayed in our communities."

What's stopping you from speaking out? Are there any fears holding you back from being more vocal about God and godly values?

_____

_____

_____

_____

_____

_____

Read John 12:42-43. What held back the religious leaders who believed in Jesus and yet remained silent?

_____

_____

_____

_____

_____

_____

The Kind of Voice We Have

Take a few minutes to reflect on 1 Corinthians 13:1, "If I speak in the tongues of men and of angels, but have not love, I am only a resounding gong or a clanging cymbal." And on Titus 3:2-5:

> . . . to slander no one, to be peaceable and considerate, and to show true humility toward all men. At one time we too were foolish, disobedient, deceived and enslaved by all kinds of passions and pleasures. We lived in malice and envy, being hated

and hating one another. But when the kindness and love of God our Savior appeared, he saved us, not because of righteous things we had done, but because of his mercy.

We don't want to be merely a clanging symbol in our society. Though we might speak loudly, we want to speak wisely and with an attitude of love and humility, remembering that we were also once people of the world enslaved to sin. We can be loud, but we can't be proud in light of God's mercy toward us and toward those who have yet to receive Him.

"As we speak up, we need to be careful to speak kindly, and without condemnation," Ron says. "We need to have a voice of compassion, not of anger. We don't finger-point and call people sinners, but we do demonstrate our love in creative ways."

Ron encourages us to break away from being on the defensive. Instead, we need to be thinking offensively about how we can be proactive and creative in bringing the culture to Christ and Christ to the culture.

Getting Creative

So how can we do this—be passionate, be vocal, be uninhibited in our faith and yet do so purely out of love and with a heart of love for people? How can we allow a righteous anger toward the world's system and the trash produced and promoted by ungodly dreamers to spur us toward action and yet keep a Christlike attitude as we go about it? How can we specifically demonstrate God's love for the youth of this generation?

All of these questions demand thought, discussion and prayer. Today, take time to ask God to give you both the boldness to speak out and the love to cover it. Actually, it's love that should embolden you, as we read in 1 Timothy and in 1 John 4:18, which says, "There is no fear in love. But perfect love drives out fear, because fear has to do with punishment. The one who fears is not made perfect in love."

Also, take time to note in the news, on the radio and on television how vocal worldly people are about their ideals, standards, politics and opinions. Let this fuel your fire for getting uninhibited and vocal about what you believe!

25

MAKING CREATIVE NOISE

So how do we make creative noise that will reshape our culture?

It starts with a dream. Please don't start out with a banner or bull-horn. Creative noise has to come out with tact and creativity, as the expression of our faith. In what area do you feel most compelled to rescue kids?

Teens can smell "corny" from a mile away and will run from it. Communication that is at once creative, authentic and sincere, however, will draw them. You don't have to try to act cool to connect with them or to impact the culture. You just have to act on the dream God has given you and do so with a pure heart. So don't worry about what others think. Your concern is in reaching them.

Creative Responses

Are you a champion of worthy causes? Do you act when you see something that's not right, or do you just have the intention of acting (or just the thought of it)? Imagine watching a woman get mugged or sexually harassed on a city street. Would you just pass by, or do something? Would you be passive, or proactive? Would you attempt to help her? When you see an accident happen or something suspicious on the side of the road, do you take out your cell phone and call 911? Do you care enough to do that, or do you leave it up to someone else? Do you take the path of action or of apathy?

Read Luke 10:30-37. In what ways can you show mercy on this generation that is daily assaulted by the media and advertising around them?

_____

_____

_____

_____

How is speaking up and taking action to bring down sexually suggestive billboards and in-appropriate sex education programs being a "good Samaritan"?

_____

_____

_____

_____

_____

When you do this, Ron reminds us, "You not only protect your kids, but you also protect the kids all over the community." Take a few minutes to answer the following questions taken from chapter 25 of *ReCreate*:

In what area do you feel most compelled to rescue kids?

_____

_____

_____

_____

_____

What, in this world, are you passionate about?

_____

_____

_____

_____

What has the Lord done in your life that engenders gratitude in your soul?

_____

_____

_____

_____

What life struggle has He brought you through?

_____

_____

_____

_____

In what area of grayness and confusion in our society do you have a clear way of communicating truth?

_____

_____

_____

_____

Where are people hurting that you could help?

_____

_____

_____

What grieves you most when you look at the struggles teens face today?

_____

_____

_____

_____

The Four Spheres of Culture

Which realm do you work best in: *entertainment, education, government or business*? Are you a writer? A photographer? An artist? A teacher? An administrator? A city official? A board member? An entrepreneur? Whatever you might be good at or do for a living or as a hobby, you have gifts and knowledge and connections in one or more spheres of society. In which could you make the greatest impact?

Do you know what YouTube is? Well, your kids most likely do, and they and their entire generation are being affected by it. Here's your homework assignment: Go online to www.youtube.com and search it out. Get informed about what's informing youth and what's transforming culture. This is now a tool for *you* to use. You, too, can be in the business of making videos—or of helping your kids make them—to funnel light through an influential cultural channel.

Perhaps you're a teacher, an administrator or on staff at a school. You have profound opportunities to impact the kids (and the parents) around you! By making your class excellent, fun and creative, and by making yourself available and approachable, you can make a mark on many students' lives in a way that no one else can.

Did you vote in the last election? Do you get involved beyond voting by volunteering to get the candidate elected who espoused godly values, or help inform others about important issues on the ballot? Why or why not?

_____

_____

_____

_____

Why is it important for Christians to make our voices heard in this manner?

_____

_____

_____

_____

If you were to run for office—even a small, local government position—what would it be and what would be your campaign positioning?

_____

_____

_____

_____

What encouragement can you get from 1 Peter 4:11 in regard to holding a public office?

_____

_____

_____

_____

Do you know who your elected state officials are and how to contact them to express your concerns about legislation? Write their names below (and if you don't know them, go online to find out).

_____

_____

_____

_____

Do you own a business? If so, what is it and how could you use it to impact the culture of your city?

_____

_____

_____

_____

_____

If you don't own a business—and even if you've never thought of owning one—write down two or three ideas of businesses you'd like to start or think would be fun to run. Go ahead, be creative! Don't be afraid to dream!

_____

_____

_____

_____

_____

Getting Creative

Write a blog. (A blog—short for Web log—is nothing more than an online journal about whatever topic you want, or about your life.) "You can choose to start a blog," Ron says, "and get people to subscribe to it so that the word spreads virtually around the Internet on issues that you may want people to engage and gather momentum for the purpose of social change."

But I don't blog! you might be thinking. True, it could be way out of your comfort zone. But what did the apostle Paul say about doing things that were out of his norm (see 1 Corinthians 9:19-23)?

_____

_____

_____

_____

_____

That's the rest of your homework for this week! Find out how to start blogging, and *do it!* Now what will you blog about . . . ?

WEEK 6

26

TEENS WHO ARE CHANGING THEIR GENERATION

Young people are rising up around the nation to take back what belongs to them. They are the Joshuas and Calebs who are "strong and courageous" and willing to fight for their generation. They are the Esthers "born for such a time as this." They are the Shadrach, Meshach and Abednegoes who would rather face the fiery furnace than fall down and worship the idols of pop culture.

Read Isaiah 58:12, Deuteronomy 31:6, Joshua 1:7 and 1 Chronicles 28:20. How can you apply these Scripture passages to the rising young generation of believers, and how can you use these words to encourage them?

_____

_____

_____

_____

Reread the examples in chapter 26 of the teen "vigilantes" who took action and confronted immorality and indecency in their communities. How do their stories inspire you to encourage your kids, and to be bold and proactive yourself?

_____

_____

_____

_____

What qualities did the teens who went to the Victoria's Secret store at the mall possess that eventually won them their victory?

_____

_____

_____

_____

_____

How were they similar to the widow's behavior in Luke 18:1-8?

_____

_____

_____

"A youth group from Arizona found out about a group that was selling what they called 'pornaments.' These ornaments were actually pornography. . . . The youth group decided to get smarter and engage the maker of these items that were being sold in stores all across the state of Arizona," Ron writes. "The youth group wrote a letter asking the company to cease from selling. The company did pull the item from their inventory, just because one youth group took action."

One youth group. Never underestimate the power of one! What might have been the result if they had held back, thinking, *What can we really do about it?* What if they had just ignored the issue and focused on other, more exciting, youth group activities?

Another testimony to the power of one is that of Zack Hunter—a young teenager who went on a crusade to end slavery. How would it make you stop and think if you saw an impassioned 14-year-old boy crying out for the oppressed in the world? How much more will people stop and take notice when young voices call out for change?

What about Michael Sessions winning mayor of his town as a 16-year-old?! Sounds like a modern-day Josiah!

Read 2 Kings 23:1-25. What did Josiah do as a young king to bring Israel back to a place of righteousness before God?

_____

_____

_____

Looking back at our stories, how do you think having such victories and testimonies empowers teens to be bold into adulthood? How does it build their faith?

_____

_____

_____

_____

_____

What can you do as an adult to encourage such faith and hope in the hearts of your teens, the teens in your church and those in your sphere of influence?

_____

_____

_____

_____

_____

_____

_____

Teens need support. They need prayer. They need mature believers who will pour into them and disciple them. They need mentors who will champion them and their cause, who won't hold them back, but rather, like Joshua, will exhort them to be strong and courageous. They need adults they can look up to who are also making a difference in their community, who are dreaming dreams, who are taking Christ to the lost and are fighting against the Machine of greed and immorality in whatever way they can. *They need you!*

Getting Creative

Gather a group of teens together and talk about the things that concern them in your city, in the media, in the nation or in the world. What injustices do they see? Where do they see others exploited or taken advantage of? What stirs up righteous anger and passion within them to see God glorified and the enemy driven out?

Talk about these things. Brainstorm and write down ideas and possibilities of how they, with your support, can make a difference in the world. As always, take time to pray at the beginning, end and throughout your meeting. Instill in them the importance of seeking God every step of the way and hearing His heart and His strategy for taking down strongholds.

ON THE OTHER SIDE OF YOUR DREAM

Now it's time to take those dreams into reality. And to keep dreaming! It's time to come alongside our young people and raise them up to be dreamers, giving them courage to go out into a world that wants to rip them apart. It's time to empower them to stand in the face of protestors shouting obscenities at them, to get them on their faces in prayer and to make a bold stance counter to the culture they're living in. It's time to *recreate* culture in our own homes, churches and communities with the intent of that culture spreading far and wide. Will you rise to the challenge? Ron exhorts us:

> I would encourage you to think that your sons and daughters are the sons and daughters of America; the ones we have been talking about throughout the entire book; the ones that are being tantalized and crushed by those who would make a profit from their destruction. These are the sons and daughters of America and the sons and daughters of the world. Our responsibility goes beyond those who live in our home to those who are living in the culture that we are allowing to flourish.

If you don't take action, think of who will. MTV and the likes will be quick to "adopt"—or enslave, rather—the kids of this generation and mold them into mooks and midriffs and people without a purpose other than to gratify themselves and make money doing it.

Revisit some of the Scripture we've studied, such as Joel 2:28, Psalm 78:1-8, Proverbs 24:11-12 and Daniel 12:3. Meditate on these passages or any other Scriptures that spoke to you while you were doing the study. Or find other Scriptures on which you can hang your vision and your dreams that inspire you. Put them around your house and remind the teens you're involved with about them. Remind yourself and them daily of God's faithfulness and of His desire to see this generation transformed for His glory. Before we ever came on the scene, He desired that this young generation would be saved and that they would worship Him (see 1 Timothy 2:1-4).

What will you do today to take steps toward your dream?

_____

_____

_____

_____

_____

What young people will you be involved with and commit to pray for and encourage?

_____

_____

_____

_____

_____

How will you make your voice heard in the battle for the hearts of this generation?

_____

_____

_____

_____

_____

Remember: You have the creative power of God and you can dream a dream that will capture the heart of a whole young generation. If the pop culture machine can dream for this generation in order to make money, can we not dream on behalf of their hearts? A dream compels people to follow. As a result, when enough people follow, it creates culture. As we dream a new dream, we *recreate* culture. A dream shows they are valued and wanted. Do we truly want them bad enough to dream? Do we want them bad enough to sweat a little (or a lot) to walk out that dream? Whoever wants them the most will win them.